Hamilton Beach Breakfast Sandwich Maker cookbook for Beginners

1000-Day Effortless Delicious Sandwich, Omelet and Burger Recipes for your Hamilton Beach Breakfast Sandwich Maker

By Sean Brandi

Table of Contents

Description

Prepare a mouth-watering, healthy breakfast sandwich in no more than five minutes!

Have you ever had a quick and fulfilling sandwich that gives the perfect blend of **flavor, crispiness, and aroma** in every morsel?

Do you love being able to combine **all** your **favorite ingredients** (meat, cheese, vegetables) in a Sandwich?

The Hamilton Beach Breakfast Sandwich Maker Cookbook is the guide to help you maximize the **crispiness** of meat, the **flavor** of the lettuce, the **fluffiness** of bread to make an **explosive sandwich.** The meals work for either breakfast, lunch, or dinner.

The recipes in this cookbook accommodate the limitations of different diet types such as Keto, Paleo, Vegan, etc. Therefore, do not fret; we have you covered. The Hamilton Beach Breakfast Sandwich Maker cookbook has a special place in your kitchen library as it contains the following information:

➢ An introduction to the Hamilton Beach Breakfast Sandwich Maker
➢ The benefits of using the Hamilton Beach Breakfast Sandwich Maker
➢ A systematic explanation of how the appliance works.
➢ Tips for Usage and Maintenance
➢ Troubleshooting
➢ *120 yummy and customizable recipes excellent for the Hamilton Beach Breakfast Sandwich Maker*

Introduction

Breakfast is the most important meal of the day. It provides the energy needed to replenish the body's loss during sleep and energizes you throughout the day. Sadly, people take breakfast meals filled with carbs, processed sugars, and fat, which are expensive and unhealthy. If you are one of these *people,* your luck is about to change because the Hamilton Beach Breakfast Sandwich Maker helps you create healthy, affordable meals at the speed of light.

Stamp out food from drives-through and breakfast meals from the diner down the street. A breakfast knight has arrived, and you are about to be saved. Equipped with the Hamilton Beach Breakfast Sandwich Maker, the recipes in this cookbook are about to save you from a lifetime of junk and convert your diet to one that satisfies both your appetite and health.

Enjoy!

Chapter 1: Fundamentals of Hamilton Beach Breakfast Sandwich Maker

What is the Hamilton Beach Breakfast Sandwich Maker

The Hamilton Beach Breakfast Sandwich Maker is a two-level homemade breakfast sandwich maker made with nonstick material. It is electrically powered, therefore, energy saving. It is a countertop appliance for indoor use only and at your discretion. In other words, you are free to use it at any time of the day and as many times as you like.

The Hamilton Beach Breakfast Sandwich Maker is rounded and bears a resemblance to the shape of English Muffins. It comprises *a base with two indicator lights (green and red) attached to it, two heating plates with handles, a removable ring assembly, and a lid.*

Besides, the Hamilton Beach Breakfast Sandwich Maker does not only make sandwiches, as you may also use it to make delicious biscuits, bagels, tortillas, and more. You are allowed to use any ingredient to maximize your satisfaction and that of your family.

The benefits of using the Hamilton Beach Breakfast Sandwich Maker

It is not enough to have the recipes, you also need to understand why the Hamilton Beach Breakfast Sandwich Maker is the perfect fit for them. Here are some of the amazing benefits of the appliance.

➢ **Easy to use and store:** Once you have your ingredients ready, all you need to do is preheat the appliance, arrange the ingredients, and then wait for the delight that ensues. The unit's compact/portable design allows it to occupy very little space while in use or storage.

- ➢ **Cleans easily:** The sandwich maker's nonstick material ensures the food does not stick to it, which makes for easy cleaning and durability. Also, the detachability of the components makes it easy to clean and dry.
- ➢ **Extremely short cooking time:** Most electric cooking appliances take at least 10 minutes to cook food. The Hamilton Beach Breakfast Sandwich Maker, on the other hand, takes just five minutes to cook a breakfast sandwich after a preheat of about two minutes. You can multitask by setting up the unit/ingredient combo and then prepare for work while your food cooks.
- ➢ **Room for recipe customization:** using the same recipes all the time tends to be boring. The Hamilton Beach Breakfast Sandwich Maker allows you to have fun by experimenting with different recipes and new ingredients to make healthy meals for you and your family.

How does the Hamilton Beach Breakfast Sandwich Maker work?

- ➢ After unboxing, the unit clean and dry before setting it up in your workspace.
- ➢ Prepare your ingredients; pre-cooked meat/bacon/chicken, bread, cheese, vegetables, and condiments.
- ➢ Plug the sandwich maker into a power source, preferably a wall socket. The red indicator light will blink-on immediately.
- ➢ Spray or lightly brush the heating plates and rings with oil or any other cooking solution you like, and close the lid.
- ➢ When the green indicator light blinks, the appliance is at the right temperature to take the ingredients.
- ➢ Place half of the English muffin or any other bread of your choice face-up on the bottom heating plate.
- ➢ Arrange the cheese, meat, lettuce, spinach on the bread. Bring down the ring and top cooking plate. Ensure you place it correctly to prevent the egg from spilling.

- Break the egg into the plate and use a fork, knife, or toothpick to disrupt the yolk.
- Cover the eggs with the other half of the bread and gently close the lid. Allow cooking for four to five minutes.
- Wear an oven mitt. Move the cooking plate clockwise by the handle until it stops.
- Use one hand to hold the bottom handle and the other to lift the ring assembly. Lift out the sandwich using a wooden, plastic, or nonstick spatula. Unplug the unit and clean when cool.
- Enjoy the meal!

Tips for Usage and maintenance

- After arranging the ingredients, do not press down the lid and avoid overloading the cooking plates to avoid spillage. Furthermore, arrange the ingredients (cheese, tomatoes, etc.) to fit in the middle of the bread, so they do not spill out to the sides. Doing this guarantees no spillage when cooking.
- Remember to preheat the sandwich maker for at least three minutes to achieve the best doneness level always.
- After the appliance is cool, detach the ring assembly for washing. Methodically wipe the top and bottom heating plates with a damp cloth or sponge, and then dry with a clean towel. Do the same for the exterior parts of the appliance.
- After washing, reattach the ring assembly through the open hinge of the base.
- Use only soft, non-abrasive materials to clean the unit.

Troubleshooting

- **Why did the bread come out too brown?** Blame this on the fat and sugar levels of your ingredients. After loading the ingredients into your sandwich maker without the coverlid down, let the eggs and other ingredients cook for some minutes without the last half of the bread. Afterward, add the bread to finish your cooking.

> **Why are the eggs overcooked?** Five minutes seems like a very short while for the food to overcook or burn, but it is possible. For eggs, the form or quantity of the eggs matters a lot. If the eggs are sized small or are just egg whites, it takes a shorter time to cook. Therefore, reduce the cooking time and adjust accordingly.

Chapter 2: Normal Breakfast Sandwiches and Omelet

Cheese, Egg and Ham Sandwich

This is one of the easiest and fastest breakfast to prepare. It is yummy and energizing. It also has a pleasant taste

Preparation time: 5 minutes

Cooking time: 5 minutes

Serves: 2

Ingredients To Use:

- 2 slices of pre-cooked ham
- 2 split muffins
- 2 big eggs
- 2 slices of cheese

Step-by-Step Directions to Cook It:
1. Preheat the Hamilton Beach Breakfast Sandwich Maker until the preheat green light is on.
2. Open the cover, the top ring, and the cooking plate
3. Put one of the split muffins at the bottom ring
4. Top with the ham and cheese
5. Lower the cooking plate with the top ring, put the egg in the cooking plate, and pierce the yolk with a fork
6. Cover with the remaining half muffin
7. Close the cover and cook for 5 minutes
8. Lift the cover and remove the sandwich

Serving suggestion: serve with juice

Preparation and Cooking Tips: use the sandwich maker according to the procedure

Nutritional value per serving: Calories: 405kcal, Fat: 21g, Carb: 30g, Proteins: 25g

South-western Muffin Breakfast

This is a pleasant breakfast meal. It is easy to make and a yummy meal.

Preparation time: 5 minutes

Cooking time: 5 minutes

Serves: 2

Ingredients To Use:

- 2 slices of Monterey jack cheese
- 2 tbsp of 20ml salsa
- 2 big eggs
- 2 split whole wheat muffin
- 6 thin slices of avocado

Step-by-Step Directions to Cook It:

1. Preheat the Hamilton Beach Breakfast Sandwich Maker until the light turns green
2. Open the cover, the top ring, and the cooking plate
3. Put the muffin on the bottom ring of the Hamilton Beach Breakfast Sandwich Maker

4. Top with the avocado and cheese, lower the cooking plate
5. Put egg white on the cooking plate, place the remaining half muffin on it
6. Close the cover and cook for 5 minutes
7. Rotate the cooking plates handle until it stops, lifts the cover, and removes the sandwich carefully

Serving suggestion: serve the sandwich with salsa

Preparation and Cooking Tips: set the sandwich maker well

Nutritional value per serving: Calories: 65kcal, Fat: 2.5g, Carb: 4.3g, Proteins: 8.6g

Bacon, Cheddar, Egg Croissant with Apple Sandwich

A combination of all these ingredients gives a sweet and yummy sandwich. It is simply amazing

Preparation time: 5 minutes

Cooking time: 5 minutes

Serves: 1

Ingredients To Use:

- 4 thinly sliced green apples
- 1 big egg
- 1 halved small croissant
- 1 pre-cooked bacon slice
- 2 tbsp of shredded cheddar cheese

Step-by-Step Directions to Cook It:

1. Preheat the Hamilton Beach Breakfast Sandwich Maker until the light turns green
2. Open the cover, the top ring, and the cooking plate
3. Put half croissant on the bottom ring of Hamilton Beach Breakfast Sandwich Maker
4. Top with bacon, slices of apple, and cheese
5. Drop the cooking plate and the top ring
6. Put the egg in the cooking plate, chop with a fork, cover with the remaining half croissant
7. Close the cover and cook for 5 minutes
8. Turn the cooking plate handle in a clockwise manner until it stops.
9. Lift the cover and the rings, serve the sandwich

Serving suggestion: serve with coffee

Preparation and Cooking Tips: follow the sandwich maker manual

Nutritional value per serving: Calories: 321kcal, Fat: 15g, Carb: 38g, Proteins: 13g

Sausage Bagel with Cheesy Egg

Cheesy egg with bagel sausage is an incredible recipe. It is delicious and has a great flavor.

Preparation time: 5 minutes

Cooking time: 5 minutes

Serves: 1

Ingredients To Use:

- 1 big egg
- 1 thinly sliced pre-cooked ham
- 1 small halved bagel
- 1 thinly sliced red pepper ring
- 1 slice of Jarlsberg cheese

Step-by-Step Directions to Cook It:

1. Preheat the Hamilton Beach Breakfast Sandwich Maker until the light turns green
2. Open the cover, the top ring, and the cooking plate
3. Put half bagel on the bottom ring of Hamilton Beach Breakfast Sandwich Maker
4. Top with red pepper meat, cheese, and sausage
5. Drop the cooking plate and the top ring
6. Put the egg in the cooking plate, chop with a fork, cover with the remaining half bagel
7. Close the cover and cook for 5 minutes
8. Turn the cooking plate handle in a clockwise manner until it stops.
9. Lift the cover and the rings, serve the sandwich with a spatula

Serving suggestion: serve with tea

Preparation and Cooking Tips: set the sandwich maker well

Nutritional value per serving: Calories: 502kcal, Fat: 27g, Carb: 54g, Proteins: 21g

Spinach, Herb Goat Cheese with Tomato Egg Breakfast Muffin

This muffin mix is an exceptional one. It is delightful and also gives food a bright morning.

Preparation time: 5 minutes

Cooking time: 5 minutes

Serves: 2

Ingredients To Use:

- 2 slices of tomatoes
- 2 split of whole wheat muffins
- 2 big egg white
- 8 spinach leaves
- 2 tbsp of herb goat cheese
- 2 thin slices of red pepper ring

Step-by-Step Directions to Cook It:

1. Preheat the Hamilton Beach Breakfast Sandwich Maker until the light turns green
2. Open the cover, the top ring, and the cooking plate
3. Put half of the muffin and goat cheese on the bottom ring of Hamilton Beach Breakfast Sandwich Maker
4. Top with red pepper ring, spinach, and tomatoes
5. Drop the cooking plate and the top ring
6. Put egg whites in the cooking plate, chop with a fork, cover with the remaining half muffin
7. Close the cover and cook for 5 minutes
8. Turn the cooking plate handle clock wisely until it stops.
9. Lift the cover and the rings, serve the sandwich by removing with a spatula

Serving suggestion: serve with fruit juice

Preparation and Cooking Tips: follow the procedure accordingly

Nutritional value per serving: Calories: 122kcal, Fat: 7g, Carb: 3g, Proteins: 14g

Sausage with Pancake Breakfast Sandwich

This is a breakfast meal that lightens the day. It gives the energy required for the day's work.

Preparation time: 5 minutes

Cooking time: 5 minutes

Serves: 2

Ingredients To Use:

- 2 big eggs
- 4 frozen pancakes
- 2 pre-cooked sausage patties
- Maple syrup

Step-by-Step Directions to Cook It:

1. Preheat the Hamilton Beach Breakfast Sandwich Maker until the light turns green
2. Open the cover, the top ring, and the cooking plate
3. Put 2 frozen pancakes on the bottom ring of Hamilton Beach Breakfast Sandwich Maker
4. Top with sausage
5. Drop the cooking plate and the top ring
6. Put eggs in the cooking plate, pierce with a fork, cover with the remaining pancake
7. Close the cover and cook for 5 minutes
8. Slide the cooking plate handle out clock wisely until it stops.
9. Lift the cover and the rings, serve the sandwich by removing with a spatula

Serving suggestion: serve with maple syrup

Preparation and Cooking Tips: treat the sandwich maker with care

Nutritional value per serving: Calories: 381kcal, Fat: 30g, Carb: 25g, Proteins: 10g

Egg, Sausage with Cheese Waffle Breakfast Sandwich

This breakfast sandwich is a pleasant and amazing one. It is not stressful to make and also has a sweet aroma.

Preparation time: 5 minutes

Cooking time: 5 minutes

Serves: 2

Ingredients To Use:

- 2 big eggs
- 3 tbsp of shredded cheddar cheese
- 2 pre-cooked sausage patties
- 4 cut in circle frozen waffles

Step-by-Step Directions to Cook It:

1. Preheat the Hamilton Beach Breakfast Sandwich Maker until the light turns green
2. Open the cover, the top ring, and the cooking plate
3. Put 2 frozen waffle on the bottom ring of Hamilton Beach Breakfast Sandwich Maker
4. Top with sausage and cheese
5. Drop the cooking plate and the top ring
6. Put eggs in the cooking plate, pierce with a fork, top with the remaining waffle
7. Close the cover and cook for 5 minutes
8. Slide the cooking plate handle out clock wisely until it stops.
9. Lift the cover and the rings, serve the sandwich

Serving suggestion: serve with cream

Preparation and Cooking Tips: use the knife to cut the waffle in a circle that fit the sandwich maker

Nutritional value per serving: Calories: 631kcal, Fat: 40g, Carb: 41g, Proteins: 25g

English Muffin Breakfast Sandwich

This sandwich is fluffy and delicious. Hamilton Beach Breakfast Sandwich Maker is the right maker to use.

Preparation time: 5 minutes

Cooking time: 5 minutes

Serves: 2

Ingredients To Use:

- 2 big egg
- 2 slices of American cheese
- 2 tbsp of green bell pepper, chopped
- 2 slices cooked
- 2 English muffins, original
- Pepper and salt

Step-by-Step Directions to Cook It:

1. Preheat the Hamilton Beach Breakfast Sandwich Maker until the light turns green
2. Mix bell pepper, pepper, egg, salt, and milk in a bowl, split the muffins
3. Lift the cover with the top ring and the cooking plate
4. Put half muffin in the bottom of the Hamilton Beach Breakfast Sandwich Maker
5. Top with pre-cooked bacon and cheese
6. Lower the top ring and the cooking plate
7. Add egg mixture and cover with the remaining muffin half
8. Close the cover and cook for 5 minutes
9. Slide the cooking plate handle out clock wisely until it stops.
10. Lift the cover and the rings, serve the sandwich

Serving suggestion: serve with maple syrup

Preparation and Cooking Tips: mix the ingredients until it is foamy

Nutritional value per serving: Calories: 133kcal, Fat: 2g, Carb: 27g, Proteins: 6g

Eggs Benedict Sandwich Breakfast and Hollandaise

This recipe is an incredible one. It is mouth-watering and also has a sweet smell. You can never go wrong with it.

Preparation time: 5 minutes

Cooking time: 5 minutes

Serves: 2

Ingredients To Use:

- 2 slices of bacon
- 2 split muffin
- 2 big eggs
- Hollandaise sauce
- 8 leaves of baby spinach

Step-by-Step Directions to Cook It:

1. Preheat the Hamilton Beach Breakfast Sandwich Maker until the light turns green
2. Open the cover, the top ring, and the cooking plate
3. Put half English muffin on the bottom ring of Hamilton Beach Breakfast Sandwich Maker
4. Top with 1 slice of bacon and 4 spinach leaves
5. Lower the cooking plate and the top ring
6. Put 1 egg in the cooking plate, pierce with a fork, top with the remaining half of 1 English muffin
7. Close the cover and cook for 5 minutes
8. Slide the cooking plate handle out clock wisely until it stops.
9. Lift the cover and the rings, serve the sandwich immediately
10. Repeat the procedure for the remaining ingredients

Serving suggestion: serve with hollandaise sauce

Preparation and Cooking Tips: rightly use the sandwich maker

Nutritional value per serving: Calories: 336kcal, Fat: 13g, Carb: 27g, Proteins: 28g

Mozzarella with Pesto Sun-dried Tomato and Egg Breakfast Sandwich

This a amazing sandwich recipe. It is very easy and quick to make.

Preparation time: 5 minutes

 Cooking time: 5 minutes

Serves: 1

Ingredients To Use:

- 1 thinly sliced mozzarella cheese
- 2 tsp of pesto
- 2 big egg whites
- 1 split whole wheat muffin
- 4 sun-dried tomatoes

Step-by-Step Directions to Cook It:

1. Preheat the Hamilton Beach Breakfast Sandwich Maker until the light turns green
2. Open the cover, the top ring, and the cooking plate
3. Put half English muffin on the bottom ring of Hamilton Beach Breakfast Sandwich Maker
4. Top with sun-dried tomatoes and cheese
5. Lower the cooking plate and the top ring
6. Put egg whites in the cooking plate, pierce with a fork, top with the remaining half muffin
7. Close the cover and cook for 5 minutes
8. Slide the cooking plate handle out clock wisely until it stops.
9. Lift the cover and the rings, serve the sandwich with a spatula

Serving suggestion: serve with cream

Preparation and Cooking Tips: place the ingredients in the sandwich maker rightly
Nutritional value per serving: Calories: 420kcal, Fat: 20g, Carb: 49g, Proteins: 18g

Grilled Cheese Sandwich

This is a crunchy and crispy sandwich. It is an irresistible and mouth-watering meal. It is a great meal to start the day

Preparation time: 5 minutes

Cooking time: 5 minutes

Serves: 1

Ingredients To Use:

- Soft butter
- 2 slices of American cheese
- 2 slices of bread

Step-by-Step Directions to Cook It:

1. Preheat the Hamilton Beach Breakfast Sandwich Maker until the light turns green
2. Open the cover, the top ring, and the cooking plate
3. Put one of the bread circle and butter on the bottom ring of Hamilton Beach Breakfast Sandwich Maker
4. Top with cheese
5. Lower the cooking plate and the top ring
6. Top with the remaining bread circle
7. Close the cover and cook for 5 minutes
8. Slide the cooking plate handle out clock wisely until it stops.
9. Lift the cover and the rings, serve the sandwich

Serving suggestion: serve the sandwich using a spatula

Preparation and Cooking Tips: cut the bread into a 4-inches circle

Nutritional value per serving: Calories: 275kcal, Fat: 15g, Carb: 27g, Proteins: 13g

Reuben Sandwich

Reuben sandwich is a mix of amazing ingredients. It gives a soft taste and melts in the mouth.

Preparation time: 5 minutes

Cooking time: 5 minutes

Serves: 1

Ingredients To Use:

- 1 tbsp of soft butter
- 2 slices of rye bread
- 1 slice of swiss cheese
- 3 slices of pre-cooked corned beef
- 2 tbsp of island dressing
- 1/3 cup of sauerkraut

Step-by-Step Directions to Cook It:

1. Preheat the Hamilton Beach Breakfast Sandwich Maker until the light turns green
2. Spread butter on one side of the bread and dressing on the other side
3. Open the cover, the top ring, and the cooking plate

4. Put one of the bread circle with butter down on the bottom ring of Hamilton Beach Breakfast Sandwich Maker
5. Top with sauerkraut and cheese
6. Lower the cooking plate and the top ring, add corned beef
7. Top with the second bread circle
8. Close the cover and cook for 5 minutes
9. Rotate the cooking plate handle clockwise until it stops, serve the sandwich immediately

Serving suggestion: serve with juice

Preparation and Cooking Tips: cut the rye bread in a circle

Nutritional value per serving: Calories: 746kcal, Fat: 50g, Carb: 40g, Proteins: 37g

Warm Breakfast Chocolate Croissant Sandwich

Chocolate croissant sandwich is a unique and amazing sandwich. It is one of the best breakfast to have

Preparation time: 5 minutes

Cooking time: 3 minutes

Serves: 1

Ingredients To Use:

- 2 tbsp of chocolate hazelnut spread
- 1 halved croissant

Step-by-Step Directions to Cook It:

1. Preheat the Hamilton Beach Breakfast Sandwich Maker until the light turns green
2. Open the cover, the top ring, and the cooking plate
3. Put half croissant with a side of chocolate up on the bottom ring of Hamilton Beach Breakfast Sandwich Maker
4. Lower the cooking plate and the top ring
5. Top with the second half of the croissant
6. Close the cover and cook for 3 minutes
7. Rotate the cooking plate handle out clock wisely until it stops.
8. Lift the cover and the rings, serve the sandwich

Serving suggestion: serve with chocolate

Preparation and Cooking Tips: cut the croissant into two halves

Nutritional value per serving: Calories: 238kcal, Fat: 14g, Carb: 26g, Proteins: 5g

Vegetarian Breakfast Panini Muffin

This vegetarian panini muffin is nutritious and delicious. It is the breakfast required for a splendid day

Preparation time: 5 minutes

Cooking time: 5 minutes

Serves: 1

Ingredients To Use:

- 1 ounce of fresh mozzarella slice
- 1 English muffin
- 1 big egg white
- 1 tbsp of black olive tapenade
- 1 ounce of roasted pepper

Step-by-Step Directions to Cook It:

1. Preheat the Hamilton Beach Breakfast Sandwich Maker until the light turns green
2. Split the muffin into 2 and spread tapenade on 1 half of the muffin
3. Open the cover, the top ring, and the cooking plate
4. Put the half muffin with tapenade up on the bottom ring of Hamilton Beach Breakfast Sandwich Maker
5. Top with roasted pepper and mozzarella
6. Lower the cooking plate and the top ring put the egg in the cooking plate
7. Close the cover and cook for 5 minutes
8. Rotate the cooking plate handle clockwise, serve immediately

Serving suggestion: serve with maple syrup

Preparation and Cooking Tips: slice the fresh mozzarella

Nutritional value per serving: Calories: 227kcal, Fat: 8g, Carb: 35g, Proteins: 13g

Breakfast Stuffed French Toast

This breakfast helps to satisfy cravings. It is one of the best breakfasts.

Preparation time: 5 minutes

Cooking time: 5 minutes

Serves: 1

Ingredients To Use:

- 1 tbsp of cream cheese
- 1 tbsp of strawberry preserves
- 1 big egg
- 1 tbsp of chopped pecans
- 1 big egg white
- 2 slices of cinnamon bread

Step-by-Step Directions to Cook It:

1. Preheat the Hamilton Beach Breakfast Sandwich Maker until the light turns green
2. Mix egg white and egg in a bowl
3. Mix pecan and cream cheese in another bowl and spread it on a slice of bread
4. Put strawberry on the second slice
5. Put the sandwich inside egg mix and soak for about 4 minutes on both sides
6. Open the cover, the top ring, and the cooking plate
7. Put the sandwich on the bottom ring of Hamilton Beach Breakfast Sandwich Maker
8. Lower the cooking plate and the top ring
9. Close the cover and cook for 5 minutes
10. Rotate the cooking plate handle clockwise, serve immediately

Serving suggestion: serve with maple syrup and confectioners; sugar
Preparation and Cooking Tips: slice the cinnamon bread in circles
Nutritional value per serving: Calories: 255kcal, Fat: 3g, Carb: 41g, Proteins: 20g

Chapter 3: Red Meat Breakfast Sandwiches and Burgers

Baked Beer Burger

The beef burger is a good meal for lunch to strengthen your day as it goes. You can never go wrong with following the right procedure for your beef burger.

Preparation time: 5 minutes   Cooking time: 10 minutes

Serves: 2

Ingredients To Use:

- ¾ envelope of dry onion soup mix
- 1 pound of ground beef
- ½ clove of crushed garlic
- ½ tbsp. of Tabasco sauce
- 2 tsp of chili sauce
- 2 buns
- Pepper
- 2 tbsp of beer

Step-by-Step Directions to Cook It:

1. Preheat the Hamilton Beach Breakfast Sandwich Maker until the light turns green
2. Mix garlic, dry onion soup, pepper, beer, tabasco sauce, and chili sauce in a bowl and set aside. Add meat and mix, shape the mix into patties
3. Open the cover, the top ring, and the cooking plate
4. Put the 1 bun on the bottom ring of Hamilton Beach Breakfast Sandwich Maker
5. Lower the cooking plate and the top ring, put the patties in the cooking plate, and cover with the second bun. Close the cover and cook for about 8-10 minutes

Serving suggestion: serve with bear

Preparation and Cooking Tips: crush the garlic cloves well

Nutritional value per serving: Calories: 191kcal, Fat: 3g, Carb: 38g, Proteins: 9g

Barbecue Quesadillas

This is the combination of various nutritious ingredients. It is a delicious and amazing burger.

Preparation time: 5 minutes

Cooking time: 5 minutes

Serves: 2

Ingredients To Use:

- ½ cup of sautéed red bell pepper
- 4 flour tortillas
- ½ cup of sautéed sliced mushroom
- 1 cup of shredded cheddar cheese
- 4 ounces of barbecued meat
- ½ cup of sautéed onion
- Barbecue sauce

Step-by-Step Directions to Cook It:

1. Preheat the Hamilton Beach Breakfast Sandwich Maker until the light turns green
2. Slice the meat and put it in a bowl, set aside
3. Mix pepper, mushroom, and onion in another bowl and set aside
4. Open the cover, the top ring, and the cooking plate
5. Put the 1 tortilla on the bottom ring of Hamilton Beach Breakfast Sandwich Maker
6. Top with sautéed vegetables, barbecued meat, barbecue sauce, and cheese
7. Lower the cooking plate and the top ring, put another tortilla on it in the cooking plate, and spray with pam
8. Close the cover and cook for about 4-5 minutes
9. Repeat the process for the remaining ingredients

Serving suggestion: serve with sour cream or salsa

Preparation and Cooking Tips: shred the cheddar cheese

Nutritional value per serving: Calories: 621kcal, Fat: 23g, Carb: 19g, Proteins: 30g

Barbecue Brisket Burger

This is a heavy burger for a busy day. It is the right meal to start the day. It gives the taste bud the feel it needs

Preparation time: 5 minutes

Cooking time: 5 minutes

Serves: 1

Ingredients To Use:

- ½ tsp of onion salt
- 1 pound of beef brisket
- ½ tsp of celery salt
- 2 ounces of barbecue sauce
- 1 ounce of liquid smoke
- 1 tsp of garlic salt
- 2 buns

Step-by-Step Directions to Cook It:

1. Preheat the Hamilton Beach Breakfast Sandwich Maker until the light turns green
2. Mix celery salt, onion salt, and garlic salt in a bowl
3. Open the cover, the top ring, and the cooking plate

4. Put the 1 bun on the bottom ring of Hamilton Beach Breakfast Sandwich Maker
5. Top with beef brisket, celery mix liquid smoke
6. Lower the cooking plate and the top ring put barbecue sauce on it in the cooking plate, and cover with the second bun
7. Close the cover and cook for about 4-5 minutes

Serving suggestion: serve with barbecue sauce

Preparation and Cooking Tips: mix the ingredients in the right proportion

Nutritional value per serving: Calories: 392kcal, Fat: 31g, Carb: 0g, Proteins: 28g

Barbecued Slaw Burgers

This is an amazing burger. It is a great meal for a special family gathering. Follow the procedure below and have the best sandwich ever

Preparation time: 5 minutes

 Cooking time: 10 minutes

Serves: 2

Ingredients To Use:

- ½ medium of diced onion
- ½ sauce of bottled water
- ½ pound of ground beef
- Coleslaw
- ½ bottle of barbecue sauce
- 2 bun halves
- 1 tbsp of brown sugar

Step-by-Step Directions to Cook It:

1. Preheat the Hamilton Beach Breakfast Sandwich Maker until the light turns green
2. Mix beef and onion in a bowl
3. Open the cover, the top ring, and the cooking plate
4. Put 1 bun on the bottom ring of Hamilton Beach Breakfast Sandwich Maker
5. Top with the beef mix, barbecue sauce, and brown sugar
6. Lower the cooking plate and the top ring, put the bun on it in the cooking plate
7. Close the cover and cook for about 4-5 minutes

Serving suggestion: serve with coleslaw

Preparation and Cooking Tips: dice the onion

Nutritional value per serving: Calories: 376kcal, Fat: 16g, Carb: 22g, Proteins: 35g

Ground Beef Burger

The beef burger is incredible. It is amazing and easy to cook. It doesn't take much time and is less stressful

Preparation time: 5 minutes

Cooking time: 5 minutes

Serves: 1

Ingredients To Use:

- 1 tsp of mustard
- 1 tsp of Worcestershire sauce
- 1 pound of ground beef
- 1 tsp of salt
- 2 tbsp of milk
- 1 tsp of catsup
- 1 split bread
- 1 small onion

Step-by-Step Directions to Cook It:

1. Preheat the Hamilton Beach Breakfast Sandwich Maker until the light turns green
2. Mix mustard, milk, onion, catsup, and salt in a bowl.
3. Open the cover, the top ring, and the cooking plate
4. Put the bread on the bottom ring of Hamilton Beach Breakfast Sandwich Maker
5. Top with ground beef and mustard mix
6. Lower the cooking plate and the top ring, put Worcestershire sauce on it in the cooking plate, cover with the other bread
7. Close the cover and cook for about 4-5

Serving suggestion: serve with cream

Preparation and Cooking Tips: chop the onion

Nutritional value per serving: Calories: 22kcal, Fat: 18g, Carb: 0g, Proteins: 22g

Beef Sandwich

The beef sandwich is irresistible. Give this mouth-watering sandwich a try.

Preparation time: 5 minutes

Cooking time: 5 minutes

Serves: 1

Ingredients To Use:

- 1 tsp of caraway seeds
- 1 tbsp of dried minced onion
- 1 tsp of dried oregano
- 1 tsp of celery seeds
- 1 pound of boneless chuck roast
- 1 tsp of salt
- ¾ tsp of cayenne pepper
- 1 tsp of dried marjoram
- Sandwich rolls
- 1 tsp of dried rosemary

Step-by-Step Directions to Cook It:

1. Mix caraway seed, minced onion, oregano, celery seed, salt, cayenne pepper, dried marjoram, and dried rosemary in a bowl.
2. Rub the seasoning over the chuck roast
3. Preheat the Hamilton Beach Breakfast Sandwich Maker until the light turns green
4. Open the cover, the top ring, and the cooking plate
5. Open the sandwich roll and put it on the bottom ring of Hamilton Beach Breakfast Sandwich Maker
6. Top with the seasoned chuck roast
7. Lower the cooking plate and the top ring, other sandwich rolls on the cooking plate
8. Close the cover and cook for about 4-5 minutes

Serving suggestion: serve with salsa or barbecue sauce
Preparation and Cooking Tips: split the sandwich roll, crush the rosemary
Nutritional value per serving: Calories: 345kcal, Fat: 15g, Carb: 35g, Proteins: 22g

Onion Marmalade and Beef Sandwich

This recipe is simply dashing, and the combination of this marmalade with beef results in an awesome sandwich.

Preparation time: 5 minutes

Cooking time: 5 minutes

Serves: 2

Ingredients To Use:

- 1 tbsp of cider vinegar
- ½ tbsp of oil
- 2 French rolls, split
- 1 green onion
- ½ cup yellow onion
- ½ tsp of Worcestershire sauce
- ½ cup of purple onion
- 1/8 tsp of pepper
- 1/8 cup of granulated sugar
- Dash ground cloves
- 2 lettuce leaves
- 1/8 tsp of salt
- ¾ pound of thinly sliced roast beef

Step-by-Step Directions to Cook It:

1. Mix Worcestershire sauce, ground cloves, sugar, pepper, vinegar, and salt
2. Sauté the onions
3. Preheat the Hamilton Beach Breakfast Sandwich Maker until the light turns green. Open the cover, the top ring, and the cooking plate
4. Open the French roll and put it on the bottom ring of Hamilton Beach Breakfast Sandwich Maker. Top with the roast beef, ground clove mix, and onion mix
5. Lower the cooking plate and the top ring, place lettuce leaves on the cooking plate, cover other French roll splits.
6. Close the cover and cook for about 4-5 minutes

Serving suggestion: serve with cream

Preparation and Cooking Tips: chop the onion, and slice the roast beef

Nutritional value per serving: Calories: 1200skcal, Fat: 70g, Carb: 88g, Proteins: 63g

Bistro Beef Sandwich

This sandwich is incredible. The beef and bread simply melt when eaten, and the taste is one to remember. Try it out now.

Preparation time: 5 minutes

Cooking time: 5 minutes

Serves: 2

Ingredients To Use:

- ½ medium red onion
- ½ pound of beef round steak
- 1 tbsp of olive oil
- 1/8 cup of dried red wine
- 1 tbsp of soy sauce
- ½ cup of sliced mushroom
- 1 clove of garlic
- ½ jar of roasted red pepper
- 2 split crusty rolls

Step-by-Step Directions to Cook It:

1. Preheat the Hamilton Beach Breakfast Sandwich Maker until the light turns green
2. Open the cover, the top ring, and the cooking plate
3. Put the half of crusty roll on the bottom ring of Hamilton Beach Breakfast Sandwich Maker
4. Top with round steak, garlic, soy sauce, red onion, sliced mushrooms, and wine mix
5. Lower the cooking plate and the top ring, put roasted pepper in the cooking plate, cover with the other crusty roll split
6. Close the cover and cook for 4-5 minutes
7. Rotate the cooking plate handle clockwise, serve immediately

Serving suggestion: serve with sauce

Preparation and Cooking Tips: cut the onion into wedges, crush the garlic and slice the mushroom

Nutritional value per serving: Calories: 365kcal, Fat: 17g, Carb: 38g, Proteins: 21g

Black Forest Beef Sandwich

This is a perfect and flavourful sandwich. It is called "Black Forest" because of the incredible combination of vegetables and sauce.

Preparation time: 5 minutes

 Cooking time: 10 minutes

Serves: 2

Ingredients To Use:

- 1 tbsp of butter
- 1/8 cup of applesauce
- Red onion, sliced
- 1/8 tsp of pepper
- 1 tsp of horseradish sauce
- ½ cup of shredded lettuce
- 2 slices of buttered rye bread toast
- Watercress
- ½ pound of flank steak
- 1 tbsp of sliced green onion
- 1/8 tsp of salt

Step-by-Step Directions to Cook It:

1. Mix horseradish, green onion, pepper, salt, and applesauce in a bowl
2. Preheat the Hamilton Beach Breakfast Sandwich Maker until the light turns green

3. Open the cover, the top ring, and the cooking plate
4. Put a slice of buttered bread toast on the bottom ring of Hamilton Beach Breakfast Sandwich Maker
5. Top with flank steak, horseradish mix, red onion, and lettuce
6. Lower the cooking plate and the top ring, put the watercress in the cooking plate, cover with another slice of buttered rye bread toast
7. Close the cover and cook for 5 minutes

Serving suggestion: serve with buttercream

Preparation and Cooking Tips: shred the lettuce and slice the onions

Nutritional value per serving: Calories: 61kcal, Fat: 2g, Carb: 2g, Proteins: 11g

Bleu Cheeseburgers

Bleu cheeseburger is a fantastic meal. It melts in the mouth, has a sweet smell and great taste.

Preparation time: 5 minutes

Cooking time: 6 minutes

Serves: 1

Ingredients To Use:

- ½ tsp of Worcestershire sauce
- 1/8 pound of bleu cheese
- ½ tsp of salt
- 1/8 tsp of hot pepper sauce
- 2 hamburger buns
- 1 tsp of ground black pepper
- 1 pound of lean ground beef
- 1 tsp of dry mustard
- 1/8 cup of fresh chives, minced

Step-by-Step Directions to Cook It:

1. Mix chives, black pepper, ground beef, salt, hot pepper sauce, mustard, Worcestershire sauce.
2. Preheat the Hamilton Beach Breakfast Sandwich Maker until the light turns green
3. Open the cover, the top ring, and the cooking plate
4. Put the hamburger buns on the bottom ring of Hamilton Beach Breakfast Sandwich Maker
5. Top with chives mix
6. Lower the cooking plate and the top ring, put the bleu cheese on it in the cooking plate, cover with the other hamburger bun
7. Close the cover and cook for about 5 minutes

Serving suggestion: serve with salsa

Preparation and Cooking Tips: coarsely ground the black pepper

Nutritional value per serving: Calories: 317kcal, Fat: 22g, Carb: 2g, Proteins: 29g

Brew Burger

Brew burger is a very special and unique burger. It has a delicious taste and a spicy smell.

Preparation time: 4 minutes

Cooking time: 6 minutes

Serves: 1

Ingredients To Use:

- 1 slice of swiss cheese
- 2 tsp of beer
- 1 split crusty whole wheat rolls
- ½ pound of ground beef
- 2 tsp of Heinz 57 sauce
- 1 small onion
- Lettuce
- Brew sauce

Step-by-Step Directions to Cook It:

1. Preheat the Hamilton Beach Breakfast Sandwich Maker until the light turns green
2. Mix brew sauce, beer, and Heinz 57 sauce in a bowl
3. Open the cover, the top ring, and the cooking plate
4. Half of the wheat roll on the bottom ring of Hamilton Beach Breakfast Sandwich Maker
5. Top with ground beef, cheese, onion, and lettuce
6. Lower the cooking plate and the top ring, add brew sauce mix to the cooking plate, cover with the other crusty wheat roll
7. Close the cover and cook for 5 minutes
8. Rotate the cooking plate handle clockwise until it stops, serve immediately

Serving suggestion: serve with sour cream

Preparation and Cooking Tips: slice the onion into a ½-inch slice

Nutritional value per serving: Calories: 690kcal, Fat: 36g, Carb: 43g, Proteins: 50g

Camel Hump

Camel hump burger is an awesome and compelling burger. It has a sweet savor. It is another creative means of making burger

Preparation time: 5 minutes

Cooking time: 6 minutes

Serves: 2

Ingredients To Use:

- 2 tomatoes
- 1 tbsp of chopped ripe olives
- 1/8 tsp of garlic salt
- 1/8 tsp of pepper
- Lettuce
- 2 tbsp of lemon juice
- 2 pita slices of bread
- 1/8 tsp of oregano
- 2 tbsp of feta cheese
- 1/8cup of Paul Masson rose
- Sliced salami
- 1/8 tsp of turmeric
- Sliced ham, cooked

Step-by-Step Directions to Cook It:

1. Mix pepper, turmeric, garlic salt, oregano lemon juice, and Paul Masson rose in a bowl
2. Preheat the Hamilton Beach Breakfast Sandwich Maker until the light turns green. Open the cover, the top ring, and the cooking plate
3. Put pita bread split on the bottom ring of Hamilton Beach Breakfast Sandwich Maker
4. Top with cheese, tomato slice, sliced salami, olive, lettuce, and pepper mix
5. Lower the cooking plate and the top ring put cooked ham in the cooking plate, cover with pita bread split. Close the cover and cook for 5 minutes
6. Rotate the cooking plate handle clockwise until it stops, serve immediately

Serving suggestion: serve with syrup

Preparation and Cooking Tips: slice the tomatoes and chop the ripe olives

Nutritional value per serving: Calories: 500kcal, Fat: 10g, Carb: 4g, Proteins: 25g

Corned Beef Sandwich

Corned beef is an exceptional sandwich. It is tempting with a sweet aroma. It is a nice meal for breakfast

Preparation time: 4 minutes

Cooking time: 6 minutes

Serves: 2

Ingredients To Use:

- ½ tsp of ground ginger
- 2 black peppercorns
- ½ tsp of red pepper flakes
- ½ tsp of dried mustard
- ½ tsp of brown sugar
- 1 bay leaf
- 1 pound of corned beef brisket
- 1 tsp of molasses
- ½ tsp of soy sauce
- 1 tsp of tomato ketchup

Step-by-Step Directions to Cook It:

1. Preheat the Hamilton Beach Breakfast Sandwich Maker until the light turns green
2. Mix mustard, soy sauce, ginger, molasses, sugar, pepper flakes, and ketchup
3. Open the cover, the top ring, and the cooking plate
4. Put bread slice on the bottom ring of Hamilton Beach Breakfast Sandwich Maker
5. Top with soy sauce mix
6. Lower the cooking plate and the top ring and put the other bread slice in the cooking plate
7. Close the cover and cook for 5 minutes
8. Rotate the cooking plate handle clockwise until it stops, serve immediately

Serving suggestion: serve with ketchup

Preparation and Cooking Tips: mix the ingredients well

Nutritional value per serving: Calories: 480kcal, Fat: 24g, Carb: 45g, Proteins: 25g

Taco Burger

The great taco burger as it depicts is incredible. It is a sweet and amazing recipe.

Preparation time: 4 minutes

Cooking time: 6 minutes

Serves: 1

Ingredients To Use:

- Lettuce
- Tortilla chips
- 1 pound of lean ground beef
- Mayonnaise
- 2 sandwich buns
- 1 ounce of taco seasoning mix
- Mustard
- Sliced tomato
- Monterey jack cheese
- Hot pepper
- Catsup

Step-by-Step Directions to Cook It:

1. Mix taco seasoning mix, mustard, Catsup, mayonnaise, tortilla chips, and hot peppers in a bowl
2. Preheat the Hamilton Beach Breakfast Sandwich Maker until the light turns green
3. Open the cover, the top ring, and the cooking plate
4. Put a sandwich bun on the bottom ring of Hamilton Beach Breakfast Sandwich Maker
5. Top with mayonnaise mix, cheese, lettuce
6. Lower the cooking plate and the top ring and put ground beef in the cooking plate, cover with a sandwich bun
7. Close the cover and cook for 5 minutes
8. Rotate the cooking plate handle clockwise until it stops, serve immediately

Serving suggestion: serve with ketchup

Preparation and Cooking Tips: slice the tomato and shred the lettuce

Nutritional value per serving: Calories: 350kcal, Fat: 15g, Carb: 20g, Proteins: 25g

Fiesta Steak Sandwich

This sandwich is palatable. It has a sweet savor. It is a low-fat meal.

Preparation time: 4 minutes

 Cooking time: 6 minutes

Serves: 1

Ingredients To Use:

- 1 tsp of lime juice
- 1 strip steak
- 1 tsp of diced cilantro
- Fiesta mayonnaise
- Tomato slices
- ½ tsp of red pepper
- 1 tsp of mayonnaise
- Avocado sliced
- 1 split hoagie roll
- Shredded lettuce
- ½ tsp of garlic powder

Step-by-Step Directions to Cook It:
1. Preheat the Hamilton Beach Breakfast Sandwich Maker until the light turns green
2. Open the cover, the top ring, and the cooking plate
3. Put 1 hoagie roll on the bottom ring of Hamilton Beach Breakfast Sandwich Maker
4. Top with strip steak, avocado, tomato, lettuce, fiesta mayo, mayonnaise, garlic, red pepper, cilantro, lime juice
5. Lower the cooking plate and the top ring, add the other split of the hoagie roll to the cooking plate
6. Close the cover and cook for 5 minutes
7. Rotate the cooking plate handle clockwise until it stops, serve immediately

Serving suggestion: serve with cream

Preparation and Cooking Tips: slice the tomato, lettuce. Shred the lettuce

Nutritional value per serving: Calories: 181kcal, Fat: 9g, Carb: 20g, Proteins: 7g

Chapter 4: Poultry Breakfast Sandwiches and Burgers

Asian Turkey Burger

The Asian turkey burger is incredible. It has a unique way of making it. It is an energizing burger

Preparation time: 5 minutes

Cooking time: 10 minutes

Serves: 2

Ingredients To Use:

- 1 egg
- 1 tbsp of teriyaki sauce
- 1 tsp of fresh ginger, grated
- 1 tbsp of water chestnut, chopped
- 1 tbsp of dried breadcrumbs
- Shredded lettuce
- 1 tbsp of French fried onions
- ½ pound of pre-cooked turkey
- 1 tsp of frank's red hot sauce
- 2 sandwich buns

Step-by-Step Directions to Cook It:

1. Mix water chestnut, French fried onion, ginger, turkey, breadcrumbs, egg, hot sauce, and teriyaki sauce in a bowl. Cut into 2 patties
2. Preheat the Hamilton Beach Breakfast Sandwich Maker until the light turns green. Open the cover, the top ring, and the cooking plate
3. Put 1 bun on the bottom ring of Hamilton Beach Breakfast Sandwich Maker
4. Top with turkey patties
5. Lower the cooking plate and the top ring, add the other bun to the cooking plate
6. Close the cover and cook for 7 minutes
7. Rotate the sandwich maker handle clockwise until it stops. Serve immediately

Serving suggestion: serve with lettuce and French fried onion

Preparation and Cooking Tips: chop the water chestnuts, grate the ginger, and pre-cooked the turkey

Nutritional value per serving: Calories: 210kcal, Fat: 3g, Carb: 6g, Proteins: 37g

Avocado with Chicken Sandwich

This is a delicious and nutritious sandwich. It is a good sandwich to start the day with.

Preparation time: 5 minutes

Cooking time: 10 minutes

Serves: 2

Ingredients To Use:

- 1 cup of shredded lettuce
- 1 ripe avocado
- 1 sliced tomato
- Black pepper and salt
- ¼ cup of jalapeno pepper, sliced
- 8 ounces of grilled chicken breast
- 2/3 cup of black beans, mashed
- 2 sandwich rolls

Step-by-Step Directions to Cook It:

1. Sprinkle pepper and salt on the avocado
2. Preheat the Hamilton Beach Breakfast Sandwich Maker until the light turns green
3. Open the cover, the top ring, and the cooking plate
4. Put 1 bun on the bottom ring of Hamilton Beach Breakfast Sandwich Maker
5. Top with sliced chicken breast, black beans, lettuce, jalapeno pepper, and tomato
6. Lower the cooking plate and the top ring, put the avocado mix in the cooking plate, cover with the other sandwich bun
7. Close the cover and cook for 5 minutes
8. Rotate the sandwich maker handle clockwise until it stops. Serve immediately

Serving suggestion: serve with ketchup

Preparation and Cooking Tips: shred the lettuce,

Nutritional value per serving: Calories: 547kcal, Fat: 28g, Carb: 56g, Proteins: 27g

Cajun Chicken Sandwich

Cajun seasoning gives the chicken so much spice and sweetness needed. It is a great sandwich.

Preparation time: 3 minutes

Cooking time: 7 minutes

Serves: 1

Ingredients To Use:

- 3 ounces of pre-cooked skinless chicken
- Butter
- Lettuce
- 1 split toasted buns
- Onion
- 1 ½ tbsp of Cajun seasoning

Step-by-Step Directions to Cook It:

1. Soak chicken inside Cajun seasoning
2. Preheat the Hamilton Beach Breakfast Sandwich Maker until the light turns green
3. Open the cover, the top ring, and the cooking plate
4. Put 1 split bun, buttered up on the bottom ring of Hamilton Beach Breakfast Sandwich Maker
5. Top with chicken
6. Lower the cooking plate and the top ring, put the other sandwich bun, buttered down in the cooking plate
7. Close the cover and cook for 6 minutes
8. Rotate the sandwich maker handle clockwise until it stops. Serve immediately

Serving suggestion: serve with lettuce, onion

Preparation and Cooking Tips: slice the chicken

Nutritional value per serving: Calories: 571kcal, Fat: 20g, Carb: 60g, Proteins: 41g

Chicken Cobb California Sandwich

This recipe is crispy and delicious. It has great flavor and a long-lasting taste. It is also nutritious.

Preparation time: 5 minutes

Cooking time: 6 minutes

Serves: 1

Ingredients To Use:

- 2 ounces of grilled boneless chicken breast
- 1 avocado
- 2 piece of fried crisp bacon
- 1 tbsp of mayonnaise
- 2 crisp lettuce leaves
- 1 ounce of blue cheese
- 1 ounce of cream cheese
- French bread loaf, split

Step-by-Step Directions to Cook It:

1. Preheat the Hamilton Beach Breakfast Sandwich Maker until the light turns green
2. Open the cover, the top ring, and the cooking plate
3. Put French bread split on the bottom ring of Hamilton Beach Breakfast Sandwich Maker
4. Top with chicken breast, blue cheese, cream cheese, lettuce
5. Lower the cooking plate and the top ring, put avocado and bacon in the cooking plate, cover with French bread loaf split
6. Close the cover and cook for 6 minutes
7. Rotate the sandwich maker handle clockwise until it stops. Serve immediately

Serving suggestion: serve with cream

Preparation and Cooking Tips: chop the lettuce and grate the cheese

Nutritional value per serving: Calories: 263kcal, Fat: 18g, Carb: 9g, Proteins: 20g

Cherry Chicken Salad Sandwich

This salad sandwich is a tempting one. It is easy to cook and ready under a few minutes

Preparation time: 3 minutes

Cooking time: 4 minutes

Serves: 1

Ingredients To Use:

- 1 tsp of lemon juice
- 1 green onion
- Lettuce leaves
- 2 tsp of mayonnaise
- 2 tbsp of dried tart cherries
- 1 croissant split
- Black pepper
- 1 cup of cooked chicken
- 1/8 cup of plain yogurt
- 1 tsp of chopped parsley

Step-by-Step Directions to Cook It:

1. Mix lemon juice, mayonnaise, pepper, and yogurt in a bowl
2. Preheat the Hamilton Beach Breakfast Sandwich Maker until the light turns green
3. Open the cover, the top ring, and the cooking plate
4. Put 1 croissant split on the bottom ring of Hamilton Beach Breakfast Sandwich Maker
5. Top with pepper mix
6. Lower the cooking plate and the top ring and put onion, chicken, and cherries in the cooking plate, cover with the other croissant split
7. Close the cover and cook for 3 minutes
8. Rotate the sandwich maker handle clockwise until it stops. Serve immediately

Serving suggestion: serve with lettuce and parsley
Preparation and Cooking Tips: cut the chicken into cubes, slice the onion
Nutritional value per serving: Calories: 230kcal, Fat: 9g, Carb: 16g, Proteins: 25g

Cordon Bleu Chicken Sandwich

This is a light and crisp sandwich with a rich flavor. It has a sweet savor and melts softly while eating.

Preparation time: 5 minutes

Cooking time: 2 minutes

Serves: 1

Ingredients To Use:

- 1 ounce of chicken patties
- 1 split buns
- 1 sliced tomato
- 1 slice of swiss cheese
- Mustard
- 1 slice of ham
- lettuce

Step-by-Step Directions to Cook It:

1. Preheat the Hamilton Beach Breakfast Sandwich Maker until the light turns green
2. Open the cover, the top ring, and the cooking plate
3. Put bun split on the bottom ring of Hamilton Beach Breakfast Sandwich Maker
4. Top with ham, mustard, tomato, and swiss cheese
5. Lower the cooking plate and the top ring, put chicken patties in the cooking plate, cover with the other bun split
6. Close the cover and cook for 2-3 minutes
7. Rotate the sandwich maker handle clockwise until it stops. Serve immediately

Serving suggestion: serve with lettuce

Preparation and Cooking Tips: slice the tomato

Nutritional value per serving: Calories: 1020kcal, Fat: 33g, Carb: 135g, Proteins: 72g

Chicken Pizza Burger

This burger has a smooth and tender texture.

Preparation time: 4 minutes

Cooking time: 8 minutes

Serves: 2

Ingredients To Use:

- 2 hot dog buns
- ½ tsp of basil
- 4 ounces of ground chicken
- 2 slices of provolone cheese
- 1 cup of pizza sauce

Step-by-Step Directions to Cook It:

1. Preheat the Hamilton Beach Breakfast Sandwich Maker until the light turns green
2. Open the cover, the top ring, and the cooking plate
3. Put hot dog bun split on the bottom ring of Hamilton Beach Breakfast Sandwich Maker
4. Top with 1 slice of provolone cheese, dried basil, and pizza sauce
5. Lower the cooking plate and the top ring and put the ground chicken in the cooking plate, cover with a hot dog bun split
6. Close the cover and cook for 5-6 minutes
7. Rotate the sandwich maker handle clockwise until it stops. Serve immediately
8. Repeat for the second bun

Serving suggestion: serve with fries

Preparation and Cooking Tips: slice the provolone cheese

Nutritional value per serving: Calories: 520kcal, Fat: 30g, Carb: 28g, Proteins: 35g

Lemony Chicken Salad Sandwich

This is a marvelous salad with nourishing flavor. The lemon gives the meal a pleasant taste and scent.

Preparation time: 5 minutes

Cooking time: 6 minutes

Serves: 2

Ingredients To Use:

- 1 tsp of lemon juice
- 2 multigrain bread, split
- 1 tbsp of mayonnaise
- 2 pound of chicken breast
- 1 tsp of fresh dill
- 2 lettuce leaves
- 1/8 tsp of salt
- 1 tbsp of plain yogurt
- 1/8 tsp of grated lemon zest

Step-by-Step Directions to Cook It:

1. Mix dill, lemon juice, mayonnaise, salt, yogurt, and lemon zest.
2. Preheat the Hamilton Beach Breakfast Sandwich Maker until the light turns green
3. Open the cover, the top ring, and the cooking plate
4. Put a slice of multigrain bread on the bottom ring of Hamilton Beach Breakfast Sandwich Maker
5. Top with lemon herb mix
6. Lower the cooking plate and the top ring and put the pre-cooked chicken in the cooking plate, cover with another slice of multigrain bread
7. Close the cover and cook for 5-6 minutes
8. Rotate the sandwich maker handle clockwise until it stops. Serve immediately

Serving suggestion: serve with lettuce

Preparation and Cooking Tips: dice the chicken and chop the dill

Nutritional value per serving: Calories: 337kcal, Fat: 22g, Carb: 14g, Proteins: 25g

Pita Taco Chicken Pockets

This is a soft and creamy bread. It has a mouth-watering taste and zesty feel. It is an amazing meal

Preparation time: 5 minutes

Cooking time: 5 minutes

Serves: 1

Ingredients To Use:

- 1 pita bread, split
- 1 small onion
- 1 tsp of lemon juice
- ¼ tsp of salt
- 2 tbsp of Monterey fack cheese, shredded
- 1 tsp of vegetable oil
- 1 tbsp of taco sauce
- ½ cup of cooked chicken
- ½ cup of shredded lettuce
- 1 ounce of green chiles
- 1 tbsp of sour cream
- 1 small sliced avocado

Step-by-Step Directions to Cook It:

1. Sprinkle salt and lemon juice on avocado
2. Mix onion, salt, chilies, oil, and chicken together
3. Preheat the Hamilton Beach Breakfast Sandwich Maker until the light turns green
4. Open the cover, the top ring, and the cooking plate
5. Put a pita bread split on the bottom ring of Hamilton Beach Breakfast Sandwich Maker
6. Top with the avocado mix, lettuce, and cheese
7. Lower the cooking plate and the top ring, put the chicken mix in the cooking plate, cover with pita bread split
8. Close the cover and cook for 4-5 minutes

Serving suggestion: serve with taco sauce and sour cream

Preparation and Cooking Tips: shred the lettuce

Nutritional value per serving: Calories: 356kcal, Fat: 5g, Carb: 50g, Proteins: 36g

Creamy Chicken Toast Burger

Creamy chicken Toast Burger is a mouth-watering adventure with a soothing taste for the mouth. You can never go wrong with the sandwich.

Preparation time: 4 minutes

Cooking time: 5 minutes

Serves: 1

Ingredients To Use:

- 1 tsp of Worcestershire sauce
- 1 package of grilled chicken breast
- 2 tbsp of shredded swiss cheese
- 1 can of condensed cream of mushroom soup
- 2 tbsp of broccoli florets
- 2 slices of bread
- 1 tbsp of milk

Step-by-Step Directions to Cook It:

1. Preheat the Hamilton Beach Breakfast Sandwich Maker until the light turns green
2. Open the cover, the top ring, and the cooking plate
3. Mix broccoli floret, mushroom soup, swiss cheese, milk in a bowl
4. Put a one bread slice on the bottom ring of Hamilton Beach Breakfast Sandwich Maker
5. Top with broccoli floret mix
6. Lower the cooking plate and the top ring, put grilled chicken breast in the cooking plate, cover with the other bread slice
7. Close the cover and cook for 4 minutes

Serving suggestion: serve with cream

Preparation and Cooking Tips: rinse the broccoli floret

Nutritional value per serving: Calories: 141kcal, Fat: 8g, Carb: 7g, Proteins: 11g

Dill Turkey Sandwich

This is a delicious, energizing sandwich. Follow the procedure and have the best meal

Preparation time: 4 minutes

Cooking time: 6 minutes

Serves: 1

Ingredients To Use:

- 2 pieces of pumpernickel bread
- 1 ½ tbsp. of non-fat mayonnaise
- 1 small red onion
- 2 sprigs of fresh dill, chopped
- 2 slices of smoked turkey breast
- 1 tsp of capers
- ¼ tsp of ground black pepper
- 3 thin slices of cucumber
- ½ tsp of dried dill

Step-by-Step Directions to Cook It:

1. Mix capers, pepper, mayonnaise, and dill
2. Preheat the Hamilton Beach Breakfast Sandwich Maker until the light turns green
3. Open the cover, the top ring, and the cooking plate
4. Put a piece of pumpernickel bread on the bottom ring of Hamilton Beach Breakfast Sandwich Maker
5. Top with caper mix
6. Lower the cooking plate and the top ring, put turkey and onion in the cooking plate, cover with pumpernickel bread
7. Close the cover and cook for about 4 minutes
8. Serve immediately

Serving suggestion: serve with cucumber

Preparation and Cooking Tips: chop the fresh dill, rinse and drain the caper
Nutritional value per serving: Calories: 325kcal, Fat: 15g, Carb: 18g, Proteins: 27g

Rachel Sandwich

This is an amazing sandwich to start the day with. It is tasteful and tender.

Preparation time: 7 minutes

Cooking time: 6 minutes

Serves: 2

Ingredients To Use:

- 4 ounces of turkey breast
- Butter
- 4 slices of dark rye bread
- 4 ounces of sauerkraut
- 4 slices of swiss cheese
- Sad dressing

Step-by-Step Directions to Cook It:

1. Preheat the Hamilton Beach Breakfast Sandwich Maker until the light turns green
2. Open the cover, the top ring, and the cooking plate
3. Put a slice of dark rye bread, buttered-up on the bottom ring of Hamilton Beach Breakfast Sandwich Maker
4. Top with swiss cheese, sauerkraut, and salad dressing
5. Lower the cooking plate and the top ring, put a turkey breast in the cooking plate, cover with a slice of dark rye bread
6. Close the cover and cook for 5 minutes

Serving suggestion: serve with cream

Preparation and Cooking Tips: slice the turkey and rinse the sauerkraut

Nutritional value per serving: Calories: 641kcal, Fat: 25g, Carb: 72g, Proteins: 43g

Reuben Chicken Sandwich

This is a nourishing and nutritional meal. It has a good savor, and it also melts on the tongue.

Preparation time: 5 minutes

Cooking time: 7 minutes

Serves: 1

Ingredients To Use:

- 1 french roll, split
- 1 cup of shredded red cabbage
- 1 small onion
- 1 boneless chicken breast
- ¼ cup of island salad dressing
- ½ cup of swiss cheese

Step-by-Step Directions to Cook It:

1. Preheat the Hamilton Beach Breakfast Sandwich Maker until the light turns green
2. Open the cover, the top ring, and the cooking plate
3. Put a split of a French roll on the bottom ring of Hamilton Beach Breakfast Sandwich Maker
4. Top with cheese, cabbage, salad dressing, onion
5. Lower the cooking plate and the top ring, put the chicken in the cooking plate, cover with other French roll splits
6. Close the cover and cook for 4-5 minutes

Serving suggestion: serve with cream

Preparation and Cooking Tips: shred the cheese, cut the chicken into half
Nutritional value per serving: Calories: 452kcal, Fat: 18g, Carb: 35g, Proteins: 45g

Jalapeno Chicken Breakfast Sandwich

This is a soft and tasty sandwich. It is a good sandwich for both winter and summer

Preparation time: 5 minutes

Cooking time: 5 minutes

Serves: 1

Ingredients To Use:

- 1/8 cup of apple cider vinegar
- 1 hamburger buns
- 1/8 cup of jalapeno jelly
- ½ tsp of salt
- 2 chicken breasts
- ½ tsp of Tabasco sauce

Step-by-Step Directions to Cook It:

1. Mix Tabasco sauce, jalapeno jelly, apple cider vinegar, and salt
2. Preheat the Hamilton Beach Breakfast Sandwich Maker until the light turns green
3. Open the cover, the top ring, and the cooking plate
4. Put a split of hamburger bun on the bottom ring of Hamilton Beach Breakfast Sandwich Maker
5. Top with tabasco sauce mix
6. Lower the cooking plate and the top ring and put chicken breast slice in the cooking plate, cover with a hamburger bun
7. Close the cover and cook for 5 minutes

Serving suggestion: serve with lettuce and tomato

Preparation and Cooking Tips: slice the chicken breast

Nutritional value per serving: Calories: 401kcal, Fat: 7g, Carb: 65g, Proteins: 30g

Hot Brown Kentucky Sandwich

This is a special sandwich. It is delicious and nutritious.

Preparation time: 4 minutes

Cooking time: 10 minutes

Serves: 2

Ingredients To Use:

- 2 tsp of grated Parmesan cheese
- 2 slices of turkey breast
- 2 tbsp of cream of chicken soup
- 2 slices of bread
- 1 tsp of light cream
- 2 slices of bacon
- 1 tsp of lemon juice
- 6 mushroom caps

Step-by-Step Directions to Cook It:

1. Preheat the Hamilton Beach Breakfast Sandwich Maker until the light turns green
2. Open the cover, the top ring, and the cooking plate
3. Put a slice of bread on the bottom ring of Hamilton Beach Breakfast Sandwich Maker
4. Top with light cream, cream of chicken soup, mushrooms, lemon juice
5. Lower the cooking plate and the top ring, put turkey breast and bacon in the cooking plate, cover with the other slice of bread
6. Close the cover and cook for 6 minutes

Serving suggestion: serve with lettuce

Preparation and Cooking Tips: slice the bacon and turkey break

Nutritional value per serving: Calories: 550kcal, Fat: 30g, Carb: 35g, Proteins: 40g

Chapter 5: Fish and Seafood Sandwiches and Burgers

Alaska Salmon Salad Breakfast Sandwich

Salmon salad sandwich is an oily sandwich. It is delicious and delightful.

Preparation time: 4 minutes

Cooking time: 10 minutes

Serves: 2

Ingredients To Use:

- 1 tbsp of lemon juice
- 1 ounce of canned Alaska salmon
- 1 tsp of plain non-fat yogurt
- 4 slices of bread
- 1 tsp of chopped celery
- Black pepper
- 1 tsp of green onion

Step-by-Step Directions to Cook It:

1. Mix green onion, celery, black pepper, yogurt. Add salmon and mix
2. Preheat the Hamilton Beach Breakfast Sandwich Maker until the light turns green. Open the cover, the top ring, and the cooking plate

3. Put a slice of bread on the bottom ring of Hamilton Beach Breakfast Sandwich Maker
4. Top with seasoned salmon
5. Lower the cooking plate and the top ring, the other bread slice on the cooking plate
6. Close the cover and cook for 8 minutes
7. Rotate the cooking plate handle clockwise until it stops, serve immediately

Serving suggestion: serve immediately

Preparation and Cooking Tips: Follow the instructions fastidiously

Nutritional value per serving: Calories: 152kcal, Fat: 12g, Carb: 5g, Proteins: 10g

Oyster Sandwich

This is a juicy and sweet sandwich. It has a distinctive taste and an exquisite flavor.

Preparation time: 4 minutes

Cooking time: 6 minutes

Serves: 1

Ingredients To Use:

- 2 sliced loaves of French bread
- ¼ tsp of cayenne pepper
- ½ tsp of baking powder
- Dill pickle slices
- Unsalted butter
- ½ dozen fried oysters in 1 tsp of cornmeal
- ¼ tsp of salt

Step-by-Step Directions to Cook It:

1. Preheat the Hamilton Beach Breakfast Sandwich Maker until the light turns green
2. Open the cover, the top ring, and the cooking plate
3. Put a slice of French bread, buttered-up on the bottom ring of Hamilton Beach Breakfast Sandwich Maker
4. Top with
5. Lower the cooking plate and the top ring, put the chicken in the cooking plate, cover with another French roll split
6. Close the cover and cook for 4-5 minutes

Serving suggestion: serve with desired sauce

Preparation and Cooking Tips: slice the cayenne pepper

Nutritional value per serving: Calories: 426kcal, Fat: 20g, Carb: 41g, Proteins: 15g

Boats Shrimps Sandwich

This sandwich has an amazing fragrance. It is a finger-licking meal.

Preparation time: 5 minutes

Cooking time: 5 minutes

Serves: 1

Ingredients To Use:

- 2 ounces of grated Cheddar cheese
- 2 ounces of cooked shrimps
- 2 thinly sliced
- 1 tbsp of mayonnaise
- 1 tbsp of minced peeled onion
- 1 tbsp of lemon juice
- 1 French bun
- ½ tsp of Seafood Seasoning, old day

Step-by-Step Directions to Cook It:
1. Mix cheddar cheese, scallions, mayonnaise, lemon juice, and seafood seasoning in a bowl
2. Preheat the Hamilton Beach Breakfast Sandwich Maker until the light turns green
3. Open the cover, the top ring, and the cooking plate
4. Put a split of French bun on the bottom ring of Hamilton Beach Breakfast Sandwich Maker
5. Top with cheese mix
6. Lower the cooking plate and the top ring and put shrimps in the cooking plate, cover with the other French bun mix
7. Close the cover and cook for 5 minutes
8. Serve immediately

Serving suggestion: serve with desired juice

Preparation and Cooking Tips: peel and devein the shrimps, peel the onion
Nutritional value per serving: Calories: 3700kcal, Fat: 180g, Carb: 455g, Proteins: 70g

Shrimps Hoagie Sandwich

This is one of the nutritional sandwiches. It is a good meal to start the day. It keeps the day bright.

Preparation time: 5 minutes

Cooking time: 10 minutes

Serves: 1

Ingredients To Use:

- 1/8 cup of butter
- 2 ounces of raw shrimp
- Pepper and salt
- 1/8 cup of olive oil
- 1 small sliced red pepper
- 2 tbsp minced garlic
- 1 small sliced green pepper
- 1 hoagie buns
- 1 tbsp crushed hot red pepper
- 1 medium onion

Step-by-Step Directions to Cook It:

1. Preheat the Hamilton Beach Breakfast Sandwich Maker until the light turns green
2. Open the cover, the top ring, and the cooking plate
3. Put a split of hoagie buns, buttered up on the bottom ring of Hamilton Beach Breakfast Sandwich Maker
4. Top with hot red pepper, onion, green pepper, red pepper
5. Lower the cooking plate and the top ring and put raw shrimps in the cooking plate, cover with hoagie buns split
6. Close the cover and cook for 10 minutes
7. Serve immediately

Serving suggestion: serve with oil

Preparation and Cooking Tips: crush the hot red pepper, slice the red pepper and the green pepper

Nutritional value per serving: Calories: 642kcal, Fat: 22g, Carb: 70g, Proteins: 50g

Shrimps Melt Sandwich

This sandwich is an energizing one. It is also finger-licking with various ingredients.

Preparation time: 5 minutes

 Cooking time: 10 minutes

Serves: 2

Ingredients To Use:

- 1/4 cup butter
- 1 tbsp of green onion, chopped
- 1 tbsp all-purpose flour
- 1 tbsp of Old Bay Seasoning
- ½ pound of shrimp
- 1 small sliced tomato
- 1 cup of milk
- 2 English muffins
- ½ tbsp. of celery
- 4 slices Provolone cheese

Step-by-Step Directions to Cook It:

1. Mix butter, flour, old bay seasoning, milk, celery in a bowl
2. Preheat the Hamilton Beach Breakfast Sandwich Maker until the light turns green
3. Open the cover, the top ring, and the cooking plate
4. Put muffin on the bottom ring of Hamilton Beach Breakfast Sandwich Maker
5. Top with butter mix, cheese
6. Lower the cooking plate and the top ring and put fresh shrimp in the cooking plate, cover with muffin
7. Close the cover and cook for 5 minutes
8. Serve immediately

Serving suggestion: serve with desired garnish

Preparation and Cooking Tips: chop the celery and green onion. Slice the tomatoes

Nutritional value per serving: Calories: 265kcal, Fat: 11g, Carb: 31g, Proteins: 17g

Italian-style Shrimps Sandwich

This is an exquisite recipe. Try it out now on your Hamilton Sandwich Maker

Preparation time: 5 minutes

Cooking time: 3 minutes

Serves: 1

Ingredients To Use:

- 1 Italian loaf of bread
- 1 small peeled avocado
- 2 ounces of Monterey jack cheese, shredded
- 1/8 pound of diced shrimp
- 1/8 cup of bottled salsa

Step-by-Step Directions to Cook It:

1. Preheat the Hamilton Beach Breakfast Sandwich Maker until the light turns green
2. Open the cover, the top ring, and the cooking plate
3. Put Italian bread loaf split on the bottom ring of Hamilton Beach Breakfast Sandwich Maker
4. Top with cheese, avocado
5. Lower the cooking plate and the top ring, put diced shrimp and salsa in the cooking plate, cover with Italian bread loaf split
6. Close the cover and cook for 3 minutes

Serving suggestion: serve with avocado

Preparation and Cooking Tips: slice the avocado, shred the cheese, and dice the shrimp

Nutritional value per serving: Calories: 260kcal, Fat: 12g, Carb: 32g, Proteins: 18g

Crab Shell Sandwich

This is a distinguish recipe with a dripping taste. It has a divine flavor that makes you want more.

Preparation time: 5 minutes

Cooking time: 5 minutes

Serves: 2

Ingredients To Use:

- 1/4 cup of flour
- 1/8 cup of tartar sauce
- ½ cup of shredded lettuce
- Seafood seasoning
- 2 sesame seed hamburger buns
- 2 soft shell crabs

Step-by-Step Directions to Cook It:

1. Coat crabs in flour and seafood seasoning
2. Preheat the Hamilton Beach Breakfast Sandwich Maker until the light turns green
3. Open the cover, the top ring, and the cooking plate
4. Put hamburger buns on the bottom ring of Hamilton Beach Breakfast Sandwich Maker
5. Top with lettuce
6. Lower the cooking plate and the top ring and put crab meat and salsa in the cooking plate, cover with hamburger buns
7. Close the cover and cook for 3 minutes

Serving suggestion: serve with tartar sauce

Preparation and Cooking Tips: shred the lettuce, thaw the crab

Nutritional value per serving: Calories: 641kcal, Fat: 37g, Carb: 48g, Proteins: 30g

Tuna Bumsteads Burger

An amazing breakfast burger with a great yummy taste. It is nutritious and easy to cook.

Preparation time: 4 minutes

Cooking time: 10 minutes

Serves: 2

Ingredients To Use:

- 1 tbsp of mayonnaise
- 2 ounces of American cheese, coarsely grated
- 1 tbsp of chopped sweet pickles
- 1 tbsp of chopped stuffed green olives
- 2 ounces of can tuna fish
- 1 hard-cooked egg, chopped
- 1 tbsp of chopped onion
- 2 buns
- 1 tbsp of chopped green bell pepper

Step-by-Step Directions to Cook It:

1. Preheat the Hamilton Beach Breakfast Sandwich Maker until the light turns green
2. Open the cover, the top ring, and the cooking plate
3. Put hamburger buns on the bottom ring of Hamilton Beach Breakfast Sandwich Maker
4. Top with cheese, green olives, chopped pre-cooked eggs, green bell pepper, onion
5. Lower the cooking plate and the top ring; put tuna fish in the cooking plate, cover with hamburger buns
6. Close the cover and cook for 10 minutes

Serving suggestion: serve with mayonnaise

Preparation and Cooking Tips: chop the pre-cooked eggs, sweet pickles, green pepper, and green olives

Nutritional value per serving: Calories: 135kcal, Fat: 16g, Carb: 40g, Proteins: 19g

Tuna Cheese Spread Sandwich

Tuna Cheese Spread Sandwich is a classic sandwich. Lemon also gives it an enticing feel.

Preparation time: 4 minutes

Cooking time: 3 minutes

Serves: 2

Ingredients To Use:

- 4 ounces of cream cheese
- ¼ cup of mayonnaise
- Bread
- 4 ounces of tuna, drained
- 1 tbsp of lemon juice
- ¾ tsp of curry powder
- ¼ cup of finely sliced scallions
- Salt

Step-by-Step Directions to Cook It:

1. Preheat the Hamilton Beach Breakfast Sandwich Maker until the light turns green
2. Open the cover, the top ring, and the cooking plate
3. Put bread on the bottom ring of Hamilton Beach Breakfast Sandwich Maker
4. Top with cheese, mayonnaise, scallion, lemon juice, salt, and curry powder
5. Lower the cooking plate and the top ring
6. Put tuna fish in the cooking plate, cover with bread
7. Close the cover and cook for 3 minutes
8. Serve immediately

Serving suggestion: serve with mayonnaise

Preparation and Cooking Tips: slice the scallion, drain the tuna

Nutritional value per serving: Calories: 100kcal, Fat: 5g, Carb: 5g, Proteins: 13g

Tuna Burgers

This is a delightful meal with a lip-smacking taste. It is a marvelous burger. It is a good burger for every season

Preparation time: 4 minutes

Cooking time: 7 minutes

Serves: 1

Ingredients To Use:

- 2 ounces of can white tuna
- ½ cup Velveeta cheese
- 1 tbsp of celery, finely chopped
- Burger buns
- 1 tbsp of chopped green olives
- 1 small onion, chopped fine
- 1 tbsp of chopped sweet pickles
- 1 tbsp of American cheese
- 1 tbsp of mayonnaise
- Pepper and salt
- 1 chopped hardboiled eggs

Step-by-Step Directions to Cook It:

1. Preheat the Hamilton Beach Breakfast Sandwich Maker until the light turns green
2. Open the cover, the top ring, and the cooking plate
3. Mix cheese, celery, green olives, onion, sweet pickles, mayonnaise, salt, and pepper in a bowl
4. Put buns on the bottom ring of Hamilton Beach Breakfast Sandwich Maker
5. Top with cheese mix
6. Lower the cooking plate and the top ring
7. Put tuna fish and chopped egg in the cooking plate, cover with buns
8. Close the cover and cook for 3 minutes
9. Serve immediately

Serving suggestion: serve with desired sauce

Preparation and Cooking Tips: chop the egg, celery, and green olives

Nutritional value per serving: Calories: 200kcal, Fat: 6g, Carb: 14g, Proteins: 26g

Crab Melt Sandwich

This is an amazing sandwich. It is the best breakfast sandwich to try. It gives you a bright day.

Preparation time: 5 minutes

Cooking time: 3 minutes

Serves: 2

Ingredients To Use:

- 1 tsp of coarse-grained mustard
- 5 ounces of fresh crab meat
- 2 tsp of grated Parmesan
- 1 tbsp of lime juice
- 2 slices of Italian bread
- ¼ cup of mayonnaise
- Unsalted butter

Step-by-Step Directions to Cook It:

1. Preheat the Hamilton Beach Breakfast Sandwich Maker until the light turns green
2. Open the cover, the top ring, and the cooking plate
3. Mix lime juice, mayonnaise, and mustard in a bowl
4. Put 1 slice of Italian bread, buttered-up on the bottom ring of Hamilton Beach Breakfast Sandwich Maker
5. Top with mayonnaise mix
6. Lower the cooking plate and the top ring
7. Put fresh crab meat in the cooking plate, cover with another slice of Italian bread
8. Close the cover and cook for 3 minutes
9. Serve immediately

Serving suggestion: serve with cream

Preparation and Cooking Tips: grate the parmesan cheese

Nutritional value per serving: Calories: 298kcal, Fat: 10g, Carb: 33g, Proteins: 22g

Crabmeat Calzones

This is also a special way of making crabmeat. It is an incredible way that does not involve stress.

Preparation time: 4 minutes

Cooking time: 10 minutes

Serves: 1

Ingredients To Use:

- ¼ pound crabmeat
- ¼ package of hot roll mix
- ¼ cup of hot water
- ¼ cup of mozzarella cheese
- 1 tbsp of vegetable oil
- 1 tsp of dried parsley
- ¼ cup of grated ricotta cheese
- 1 clove of minced garlic
- 4 ounces of cream cheese, softened
- 2 chopped green onions
- 1 small can of olives

Step-by-Step Directions to Cook It:

1. Mix hot roll mix with hot water and stir until it forms a fine dough
2. Preheat the Hamilton Beach Breakfast Sandwich Maker until the light turns green
3. Open the cover, the top ring, and the cooking plate
4. Put half dough on the bottom ring of Hamilton Beach Breakfast Sandwich Maker
5. Top with cheese, onion, garlic, glove, and parsley
6. Lower the cooking plate and the top ring
7. Put crabmeat in the cooking plate, cover with dough
8. Close the cover and cook for 3 minutes
9. Serve immediately

Serving suggestion: serve with the desired cram

Preparation and Cooking Tips: chop the olives, grate the cheese

Nutritional value per serving: Calories: 195kcal, Fat: 7g, Carb: 30g, Proteins: 10g

Salmon Burger

This is a spicy and tantalizing burger. It is irresistible when making it. It has a sweet taste and a captivating scent.

Preparation time: 5 minutes

Cooking time: 3 minutes

Serves: 1

Ingredients To Use:

- 2 ounces of salmon
- 1/6 cup of chopped onions
- 1 tbsp of mayonnaise
- 1 egg
- 1/8 cup of uncooked oatmeal
- 1 tsp of horseradish
- ¼ cup of cornflake crumbs
- 1 tbsp of lemon juice

Step-by-Step Directions to Cook It:

1. Mix oatmeal, corn flakes crumbs, mayonnaise, onion, and lemon juice.
2. Form patties from the mixture
3. Preheat the Hamilton Beach Breakfast Sandwich Maker until the light turns green
4. Open the cover, the top ring, and the cooking plate
5. Put patties on the bottom ring of Hamilton Beach Breakfast Sandwich Maker
6. Lower the cooking plate and the top ring
7. Put salmon and egg in the cooking plate, cover with another patty
8. Close the cover and cook for 5 minutes
9. Serve immediately

Serving suggestion: serve with horseradish sauce

Preparation and Cooking Tips: chop the onion and use uncooked oatmeal

Nutritional value per serving: Calories: 497kcal, Fat: 30g, Carb: 17g, Proteins: 46g

Lobster Sandwich

The lobster sandwich is a great recipe with special ingredients. It gives the taste bud the desired feel.

Preparation time: 4 minutes

Cooking time: 5 minutes

Serves: 1

Ingredients To Use:

- ½ pound of lobster
- 2 slices bacon
- 1 tbsp lemon
- 4 slices of tomato
- mayonnaise
- 2 slices brioche
- 1/8 cup of sliced mixed field greens

Step-by-Step Directions to Cook It:

1. Preheat the Hamilton Beach Breakfast Sandwich Maker until the light turns green
2. Open the cover, the top ring, and the cooking plate
3. Put a slice of brioche on the bottom ring of Hamilton Beach Breakfast Sandwich Maker
4. Top with mayonnaise, mixed field greens, tomatoes
5. Lower the cooking plate and the top ring, put lobster and bacon in the cooking plate, cover with another slice of brioche
6. Close the cover and cook for 5 minutes
7. Serve immediately

Serving suggestion: serve with cream

Preparation and Cooking Tips: slice the bacon

Nutritional value per serving: Calories: 1061kcal, Fat: 57g, Carb: 110g, Proteins: 31g

Acapulco Fish Burgers

As a food lover, this is a meal that satisfies cravings. It is a mouth-watering recipe

Preparation time: 4 minutes

Cooking time: 5 minutes

Serves: 2

Ingredients To Use:

- 1 pound of fish fillets
- 3 tbsp of shortening
- 1 medium of chopped green bell pepper
- 2 cups of soft bread crumbs
- ¼ tsp of pepper
- 2 medium of onions, chopped
- ¾ tsp of salt

Step-by-Step Directions to Cook It:

1. Preheat the Hamilton Beach Breakfast Sandwich Maker until the light turns green
2. Open the cover, the top ring, and the cooking plate
3. Mix onion, pepper, green pepper, bread crumbs, and salt in a bowl.
4. Form patties from the mix
5. Put patties on the bottom ring of Hamilton Beach Breakfast Sandwich Maker
6. Lower the cooking plate and the top ring, put fish fillets in the cooking plate, cover the fish with patties
7. Close the cover and cook for 5 minutes
8. Serve immediately

Serving suggestion: serve with whipped cream

Preparation and Cooking Tips: chop the onion and the green bell pepper

Nutritional value per serving: Calories: 355kcal, Fat: 3g, Carb: 43g, Proteins: 32g

Chapter 6: Vegan and Vegetarian Sandwich and Omelettes

Avocado Lettuce Sandwich

This recipe is designed for a celebration or family gathering. It tastes incredible and deserves to be eaten with friends. Invite them over for a delightful combination of cilantro, salsa, jack cheese, tomato, and many more.

Preparation time: 10 minutes
Cooking time: 30 minutes
Serves: 12

Ingredients To Use:

- 24 slices sliced Jalapeno Jack cheese
- 12 sprigs of cilantro, chopped
- 3/4 cup of aioli garlic mayonnaise
- 3 cups of fresh fruit salsa, any fruit you desired
- 24 slices of firm white sandwich bread
- 6 California avocados, sliced
- 6, cherry tomatoes, sliced into rounds
- 24 lettuce leaves

Step-by-Step Directions to Cook It:

1. Preheat the Hamilton Beach Breakfast Sandwich Maker until the light turns green. Open the cover, the top ring, and the cooking plate
2. Butter all 12 slices of bread with the garlic mayonnaise
3. Put a slice of bread on the bottom ring of Hamilton Beach Breakfast Sandwich Maker
4. Top with a lettuce leaf, avocado slices, tomato slices, a cheese slice, sprinkles of cilantro, and another lettuce leaf
5. Lower the cooking plate and the top ring, the other bread slice on the cooking plate. Close the cover and cook for 3 minutes
6. Rotate the cooking plate handle clockwise until it stops.
7. Repeat the process until the bread, and other ingredients are exhausted.

Serving suggestion: serve with fresh fruit salsa
Preparation and Cooking Tips: Follow the instructions fastidiously
Nutritional value per serving: Calories: 112kcal, Fat: 8g, Carb: 5g, Proteins: 6g

Avocado Hamilton Muffins

Have a splendid day with this incredibly prepared English Muffin. The ingredients combine to produce great flavor.

Preparation time: 5 minutes
Cooking time: 3 minutes
Serves: 2

Ingredients To Use:
- 11/3 cups of Monterey jack cheese, coarsely grated
- 3 Tbsp of chopped cilantro, fresh
- 1 avocado, peeled and sliced
- 1/4 tsp of Tabasco sauce
- Cherry tomatoes, sliced into rounds
- 1 Tbsp of chopped red onions
- 4 English Muffin halves

Step-by-Step Directions to Cook It:

1. Preheat the Hamilton Beach Breakfast Sandwich Maker until the light turns green
2. Open the cover, the top ring, and the cooking plate
3. Put a muffin half on the bottom ring of Hamilton Beach Breakfast Sandwich Maker
4. Top with avocado slices, tomato slices, chopped onions, a heavy sprinkle of cheese, and cilantro.
5. Brush the toppings with Tabasco sauce
6. Lower the cooking plate and the top ring, the other muffin half on the cooking plate
7. Close the cover and cook for 3 minutes
8. Rotate the cooking plate handle clockwise until it stops, serve immediately

Serving suggestion: serve with fresh orange juice
Preparation and Cooking Tips: Follow the instructions fastidiously
Nutritional value per serving: Calories: 132kcal, Fat: 9g, Carb: 4g, Proteins: 7g

Slaw Muffins

Slaw Muffin is simple and very easy to prepare. Despite having a small combination of ingredients, it tastes amazing

Preparation time: 5 minutes
Cooking time: 3 minutes
Serves: 2

Ingredients To Use:
- ½ medium of diced onion
- 1 Tbsp of Chocolate spread
- Coleslaw
- 2 English muffin halves

Step-by-Step Directions to Cook It:
1. Preheat the Hamilton Beach Breakfast Sandwich Maker until the light turns green
2. Open the cover, the top ring, and the cooking plate
3. Butter the muffin halves with the chocolate spread
4. Put 1 muffin half on the bottom ring of Hamilton Beach Breakfast Sandwich Maker
5. Top with the diced onion and coleslaw
6. Lower the cooking plate and the top ring, add the other muffin half to the cooking plate
7. Close the cover and cook for about 3 minutes

Serving suggestion: serve with fresh pineapple juice
Preparation and Cooking Tips: Follow the instructions fastidiously
Nutritional value per serving: Calories: 116kcal, Fat: 9g, Carb: 4g, Proteins: 7g

Hamilton Cheese Sandwich

Taste greatness with this traditional cheese recipe. It is simple, delicious, and filling

Preparation time: 5 minutes
Cooking time: 3 minutes
Serves: 1

Ingredients To Use:

- 1 Tbsp of Chocolate spread
- 2 slices of bread
- 2 Tbsp cornmeal
- 1 tsp of ground cinnamon
- 2 Tbsp of grated parmesan cheese
- 1 Cherry tomato, sliced into rounds
- 1 fresh mushroom chopped

Step-by-Step Directions to Cook It:

1. . Preheat the Hamilton Beach Breakfast Sandwich Maker until the light turns green
2. Open the cover, the top ring, and the cooking plate
3. Butter the bread slices with the chocolate spread
4. Put 1 bread slice on the bottom ring of Hamilton Beach Breakfast Sandwich Maker
5. Top with the cornmeal, cinnamon, cheese, tomato slices, and chopped mushroom
6. Lower the cooking plate and the top ring, add the other bread to the cooking plate
7. Close the cover and cook for about 3 minutes

Serving suggestion: serve immediately
Preparation and Cooking Tips: Follow the instructions fastidiously
Nutritional value per serving: Calories: 121kcal, Fat: 7g, Carb: 6g, Proteins: 5g

Jack Sandwich

This sandwich is bound to get you addicted. Try it now with your Hamilton Beach Breakfast Sandwich Maker

Preparation time: 5 minutes
Cooking time: 24 minutes
Serves: 12

Ingredients To Use:

- 8 buns
- 2 tbsp of diced onion
- 2 Tbsp of vegan mayonnaise
- 1/2 teaspoon cayenne pepper
- 1 garlic clove, diced
- 6 ounces of pre-made vegetable slaw
- 1/4 teaspoon red pepper flakes
- 28 ounces of jackfruit, rinsed and chopped
- Black pepper, as desired

Step-by-Step Directions to Cook It:

1. Preheat the Hamilton Beach Breakfast Sandwich Maker until the light turns green
2. Open the cover, the top ring, and the cooking plate
3. Butter the bun with vegan mayonnaise.
4. Put 1 bun half on the bottom ring of Hamilton Beach Breakfast Sandwich Maker
5. Top with the onions, vegetable slaw, jack fruit, red pepper flakes, garlic, cayenne pepper, and black pepper.
6. Lower the cooking plate and the top ring, add the other bun to the cooking plate
7. Close the cover and cook for about 4 minutes
8. Repeat until bread is exhausted

Serving suggestion: serve immediately
Preparation and Cooking Tips: Follow the instructions fastidiously
Nutritional value per serving: Calories: 113kcal, Fat: 5g, Carb: 4g, Proteins: 2g

BLT Sandwich

Impress your friends with this amazing recipe. It is delicious, quick, and pleasing to the eyes.

Preparation time: 5 minutes
Cooking time: 4 minutes
Serves: 1

Ingredients To Use:
- 2 slices of Vegan Bread
- 6 slices of Eggplant bacon
- 2 Tbsp of Hummus
- 1/4 medium white onion, sliced
- 1/2 ripe tomato, sliced into rounds
- 2 green lettuce leaves

Step-by-Step Directions to Cook It:
1. Preheat the Hamilton Beach Breakfast Sandwich Maker until the light turns green
2. Open the cover, the top ring, and the cooking plate
3. Put 1 bread slice on the bottom ring of Hamilton Beach Breakfast Sandwich Maker
4. Top with the lettuce leaf, onions, eggplant bacon, tomato slices, hummus, and cover with the other lettuce leaf
5. Lower the cooking plate and the top ring, add the other bread slice to the cooking plate
6. Close the cover and cook for about 3 minutes

Serving suggestion: serve immediately

Preparation and Cooking Tips: Follow the instructions fastidiously

Nutritional value per serving: Calories: 131kcal, Fat: 8g, Carb: 5g, Proteins: 3g

Reuben Vegan Sandwich

Feast with this amazing delicacy. It contains rich ingredients, and the taste is sure to brighten your day.

Preparation time: 5 minutes
Cooking time: 8 minutes
Serves: 2

Ingredients To Use:
- Black pepper, as desired
- 1 Tbsp of mustard seeds
- 4 slices of rye bread
- 2 Tbsp of organic butter
- 1/4 cup of cashew cheese
- 1 cup of sauerkraut
- 2 slices of swiss cheese

Step-by-Step Directions to Cook It:

1. Preheat the Hamilton Beach Breakfast Sandwich Maker until the light turns green
2. Open the cover, the top ring, and the cooking plate
3. Butter the bread with organic butter.
4. Put 1 bread slice on the bottom ring of Hamilton Beach Breakfast Sandwich Maker
5. Top with the mustard seed, cashew cheese, sauerkraut, and swiss cheese
6. Lower the cooking plate and the top ring, add the other bread slice to the cooking plate
7. Close the cover and cook for about 4 minutes
8. Repeat until bread is exhausted

Serving suggestion: serve immediately
Preparation and Cooking Tips: Follow the instructions fastidiously
Nutritional value per serving: Calories: 115kcal, Fat: 5g, Carb: 2g, Proteins: 1g

Hamilton Chive Sandwich

Start your day with this remarkable chive sandwich. It takes great, smells great, and cooks fast when prepared with the Hamilton Beach Breakfast Sandwich Maker

Preparation time: 5 minutes
Cooking time: 8 minutes
Serves: 2

Ingredients To Use:
- 4 lettuce leaves
- 2 tbsp vegan mayonnaise
- 2 tsp finely chopped chives
- ¼ tsp ground turmeric
- ½ tsp Dijon mustard
- 4 slices of large white sandwich

Step-by-Step Directions to Cook It:

1. Preheat the Hamilton Beach Breakfast Sandwich Maker until the light turns green
2. Open the cover, the top ring, and the cooking plate
3. Butter the bread with the vegan mayonnaise
4. Put 1 bread slice on the bottom ring of Hamilton Beach Breakfast Sandwich Maker
5. Top with the lettuce leaf, chopped chives, turmeric, Dijon mustard, and cover with a lettuce leaf
6. Lower the cooking plate and the top ring, add the other bread slice to the cooking plate
7. Close the cover and cook for about 4 minutes
8. Repeat until bread is exhausted

Serving suggestion: serve immediately
Preparation and Cooking Tips: Follow the instructions fastidiously
Nutritional value per serving: Calories: 139kcal, Fat: 5g, Carb: 18g, Proteins: 5g

Green Sandwich

Filled with the right amount of vegetables, Green Sandwich delivers both nutrients and taste.

Preparation time: 5 minutes

Cooking time: 4 minutes

Serves: 1

Ingredients To Use:

- ½ tsp paprika
- 2 curly kale leaves, chopped
- ½ cup of chickpeas
- ½ tbsp sesame oil
- 2 slices rye bread
- ½ tbsp tamari
- 1 small avocado, sliced.

Step-by-Step Directions to Cook It:

1. Preheat the Hamilton Beach Breakfast Sandwich Maker until the light turns green
2. Open the cover, the top ring, and the cooking plate
3. Put 1 bread slice on the bottom ring of Hamilton Beach Breakfast Sandwich Maker
4. Top with the kale leaves, avocado slices, tamari, sesame oil, chickpeas, and paprika.
5. Lower the cooking plate and the top ring, add the other bread slice to the cooking plate
6. Close the cover and cook for about 4 minutes. Repeat until bread is exhausted

Serving suggestion: serve immediately

Preparation and Cooking Tips: Follow the instructions fastidiously

Nutritional value per serving: Calories: 139kcal, Fat: 5g, Carb: 18g, Proteins: 5g

Beet Root Sandwich

Beet is a great antioxidant, and its inclusion in this recipe makes it a great meal to start your day

Preparation time: 5 minutes
Cooking time: 4 minutes
Serves: 1

Ingredients To Use:
- 2 large handfuls of mixed watercress, rocket, and spinach salad
- ½ cup can chickpeas
- 3 tbsp of vegan pesto
- olive oil, as desired
- 1 whole beetroot, cooked, chopped
- Splash of vinegar
- 2 medium ciabatta rolls, cut in half

Step-by-Step Directions to Cook It:

1. Preheat the Hamilton Beach Breakfast Sandwich Maker until the light turns green
2. Open the cover, the top ring, and the cooking plate
3. Put 1 ciabatta roll on the bottom ring of Hamilton Beach Breakfast Sandwich Maker
4. Top with the beets, chickpeas, pesto, olive oil, vinegar, and salad.
5. Lower the cooking plate and the top ring, add the other ciabatta roll to the cooking plate
6. Close the cover and cook for about 4 minutes

Serving suggestion: serve immediately
Preparation and Cooking Tips: Follow the instructions fastidiously
Nutritional value per serving: Calories: 122kcal, Fat: 5g, Carb: 15g, Proteins: 5g

Tila Sandwich

A great sandwich meal that is capable of transforming your stressful day into an enjoyable one.

Preparation time: 5 minutes
Cooking time: 8 minutes
Serves: 2

Ingredients To Use:
- Dill pickles, chopped
- Pre-made Garlic Aioli
- 4 bread slices
- 1 cherry tomato, cut into slices
- 1 avocado, peeled and sliced
- Baby romaine, chopped

Step-by-Step Directions to Cook It:

1. Preheat the Hamilton Beach Breakfast Sandwich Maker until the light turns green
2. Open the cover, the top ring, and the cooking plate
3. Put 1 bread slice on the bottom ring of Hamilton Beach Breakfast Sandwich Maker
4. Top with pickles, romaine leaves, garlic aioli, tomato slices, and avocado.
5. Lower the cooking plate and the top ring, add the other bread slice to the cooking plate
6. Repeat until bread is exhausted
7. Close the cover and cook for about 4 minutes

Serving suggestion: serve immediately
Preparation and Cooking Tips: Follow the instructions fastidiously
Nutritional value per serving: Calories: 119kcal, Fat: 5g, Carb: 12g, Proteins: 5g

Vegan Philly Sandwich

This recipe is great for weight loss and can serve your needs all day long.

Preparation time: 5 minutes
Cooking time: 4 minutes
Serves: 1

Ingredients To Use:

- ½ poblano pepper, chopped
- 2 hoagie rolls
- salt and pepper, as desired
- 4 portobellos, chopped
- 1 green bell pepper, chopped
- 1 yellow onion, chopped
- 1 cup of sliced button mushrooms

Step-by-Step Directions to Cook It:

1. Preheat the Hamilton Beach Breakfast Sandwich Maker until the light turns green
2. Open the cover, the top ring, and the cooking plate
3. Put 1 hoagie half on the bottom ring of Hamilton Beach Breakfast Sandwich Maker
4. Top with the portobellos, onion, bell pepper, poblano, mushroom.
5. Season with salt and pepper.
6. Lower the cooking plate and the top ring, add the other hoagie roll to the cooking plate
7. Close the cover and cook for about 4 minutes

Serving suggestion: serve immediately

Preparation and Cooking Tips: Follow the instructions fastidiously

Nutritional value per serving: Calories: 124kcal, Fat: 5g, Carb: 12g, Proteins: 5g

Peanut Veggie Sandwich

This meal delivers all the rich, delicious goodness you need from a sandwich. Try it out now on your Hamilton Beach Breakfast Sandwich Maker

Preparation time: 5 minutes
Cooking time: 8 minutes
Serves: 2

Ingredients To Use:
- ½ cup of purple cabbage
- ¼ cup of peanut butter
- ½ cup of chopped cilantro
- 2 tsp of hoisin sauce
- 2 tsp of sriracha
- 2 tsp of soy sauce
- 2 French baguette rolls, halved
- ½ cup of white onion
- ½ cup of sliced cucumber
- ½ cup of red bell pepper

Step-by-Step Directions to Cook It:

1. Preheat the Hamilton Beach Breakfast Sandwich Maker until the light turns green
2. Open the cover, the top ring, and the cooking plate
3. Butter the rolls with the peanut butter
4. Put 1 half roll on the bottom ring of Hamilton Beach Breakfast Sandwich Maker
5. Top with the purple cabbage, cilantro, hoisin sauce, sriracha, soy, white onion, bell pepper, and cucumber.
6. Lower the cooking plate and the top ring, add the other bread slice to the cooking plate
7. Close the cover and cook for about 4 minutes
8. Repeat until bread is exhausted

Serving suggestion: serve immediately
Preparation and Cooking Tips: Follow the instructions fastidiously
Nutritional value per serving: Calories: 131kcal, Fat: 5g, Carb: 13g, Proteins: 5g

Vegan Sloppy Joes

This recipe is an absolute delight. It is incredibly filling and is full of flavors.

Preparation time: 5 minutes
Cooking time: 8 minutes
Serves: 2

Ingredients To Use:

- 1 tsp brown sugar, as desired
- 4 sandwich buns
- 1 Tbsp of olive oil
- salt, as desired
- ½ onion, chopped
- ½ cup of chickpeas
- 2 garlic cloves, grated
- ½ green bell pepper, chopped
- ½ cup of organic ketchup
- 1 tsp of yellow mustard
- 4 ounces of tomato sauce

Step-by-Step Directions to Cook It:

1. Preheat the Hamilton Beach Breakfast Sandwich Maker until the light turns green
2. Open the cover, the top ring, and the cooking plate
3. Mix the oil, chickpeas, garlic, ketchup, salt, onion, and tomato sauce in a bowl.
4. Put 1 bun half on the bottom ring of Hamilton Beach Breakfast Sandwich Maker
5. Top the bread half with the tomato mix and drizzle with yellow mustard.
6. Lower the cooking plate and the top ring, add the other bread slice to the cooking plate
7. Close the cover and cook for about 4 minutes
8. Repeat until bread is exhausted

Serving suggestion: serve immediately
Preparation and Cooking Tips: Follow the instructions fastidiously
Nutritional value per serving: Calories: 142kcal, Fat: 7g, Carb: 12g, Proteins: 11g

Coconut Peach Sandwich

Start your day with this remarkable chive sandwich. It takes great, smells great, and cooks fast when prepared with the Hamilton Beach Breakfast Sandwich Maker

Preparation time: 5 minutes
Cooking time: 16 minutes
Serves: 4

Ingredients To Use:

- 4 tsp of maple syrup
- 1 cup of unsweetened coconut flakes
- 1/2 tsp of onion powder
- 3/4 tsp of sea salt
- 1/2 tsp of garlic powder
- 1/8 tsp of ground black pepper
- 1/4 tsp of smoked paprika

- 8 slices of sourdough bread
- 8 leaves of lettuce
- 5 Tbsp of vegan mayo
- 1 large tomato, sliced
- ¾ cup of Coconut Bacon
- 1 cup of sliced peaches
- 1/8 tsp of ground black pepper

Step-by-Step Directions to Cook It:

1. Preheat the Hamilton Beach Breakfast Sandwich Maker until the light turns green
2. Open the cover, the top ring, and the cooking plate
3. Butter the bread with maple syrup and vegan mayo
4. Put 1 bread slice on the bottom ring of Hamilton Beach Breakfast Sandwich Maker
5. Top with the lettuce leaf, peaches, coconut bacon, black pepper, tomato slices, coconut flakes, onion powder, garlic powder, paprika, and sprinkle with sea salt.
6. Cover with a lettuce leaf.
7. Lower the cooking plate and the top ring, add the other bread slice to the cooking plate
8. Close the cover and cook for about 4 minutes
9. Repeat until bread is exhausted

Serving suggestion: serve immediately
Preparation and Cooking Tips: Follow the instructions fastidiously
Nutritional value per serving: Calories: 139kcal, Fat: 5g, Carb: 18g, Proteins: 5g

Chapter 7: Gluten-Free Sandwich and Burgers

Chicken Salad Sandwich

Eat healthily and deliciously with this incredible recipe. Chicken Salad Sandwich is simple yet flavor-rich.

Preparation time:5 minutes

Cooking time: 4 minutes

Serves: 1

Ingredients To Use:

- 2 slices of gluten-free Bread
- 2 tsp of gluten-free egg mayonnaise
- 1/2 cup of shredded chicken breast fillet, cooked
- 1/4 cup of grated carrot
- 4 baby spinach leaves

Step-by-Step Directions to Cook It:

1. Preheat the Hamilton Beach Breakfast Sandwich Maker until the light turns green
2. Open the cover, the top ring, and the cooking plate
3. Butter all 12 slices of bread with the egg mayonnaise
4. Put a slice of bread on the bottom ring of Hamilton Beach Breakfast Sandwich Maker
5. Top with the spinach leaves, grated carrots, and chicken.
6. Top again with spinach leaves
7. Lower the cooking plate and the top ring, the other bread slice on the cooking plate. Close the cover and cook for 3 minutes

Serving suggestion: serve with fruit juice

Preparation and Cooking Tips: Follow the instructions fastidiously

Nutritional value per serving: Calories: 156kcal, Fat: 15g, Carb: 21g, Proteins: 16g

Club Sandwich

Premium meals do not always have to be complicated; this Club Sandwich recipe is proof of that. Try it out now

Preparation time: 5 minutes

 Cooking time: 4 minutes

Serves: 1

Ingredients To Use:

- 3 slices of Gluten-Free Bread
- 2 slices of swiss cheese
- 1 tbsp of Mayo
- Lettuce and other greens, a handful
- 2 slices of smoked turkey
- 2 slices of black forest ham
- 2 slices of cooked bacon

Step-by-Step Directions to Cook It:

1. Preheat the Hamilton Beach Breakfast Sandwich Maker until the light turns green
2. Open the cover, the top ring, and the cooking plate
3. Put a slice of bread on the bottom ring of Hamilton Beach Breakfast Sandwich Maker

4. Top with the greens, smoked turkey, mayo, and swiss cheese.

5. Add another bread and top with black forest ham, and bacon

6. Lower the cooking plate and the top ring, the other bread slice on the cooking plate

7. Close the cover and cook for 3 minutes

Serving suggestion: serve with orange juice

Preparation and Cooking Tips: Follow the instructions fastidiously

Nutritional value per serving: Calories: 718kcal, Fat: 45g, Carb: 28g, Proteins: 49g

Triple-Treat Gluten-Free Sandwich

This is one of the most delicious and power-packed recipes possible of the Hamilton Beach Breakfast Sandwich Maker It has so many delightful ingredients, and it tastes amazing.

Preparation time: 10 minutes

Cooking time: 4 minutes

Serves: 1

Ingredients To Use:

- 2 slices of gluten-free bread
- mayo, as desired
- 3 thin slices of smoked turkey
- mustard, as desired
- 2 lettuce leaves
- 1 slice of sharp cheddar cheese
- 2 slices of smoked ham
- 2 slices of roast beef
- 2 slices of parmesan cheese
- 3 slices tomato

Step-by-Step Directions to Cook It:

1. Preheat the Hamilton Beach Breakfast Sandwich Maker until the light turns green
2. Open the cover, the top ring, and the cooking plate
3. Put a slice of bread on the bottom ring of Hamilton Beach Breakfast Sandwich Maker

4. Top with the spinach leaf, ham, beef, tomato slices, turkey, mayo, mustard, parmesan cheese, jack cheese, and lettuce leaf.

5. Lower the cooking plate and the top ring, the other bread slice on the cooking plate. Close the cover and cook for 3 minutes

Serving suggestion: serve with fruit juice

Preparation and Cooking Tips: Follow the instructions fastidiously

Nutritional value per serving: Calories: 256kcal, Fat: 25g, Carb: 31g, Proteins: 26g

Traditional Sandwich

This recipe is made amazing by the Hamilton Beach Breakfast Sandwich Maker

Preparation time: 5 minutes

Cooking time: 24 minutes

Serves: 6

Ingredients To Use:

- 12 slices of gluten-free Bread
- 2 medium eggs
- 1 tbsp of mayonnaise
- ½ punnet salad cress
- 5 Tbsp of butter
- 1 smoked salmon, shredded
- 3 tbsp of cream cheese
- ½ lemon, juiced

Step-by-Step Directions to Cook It:

1. Preheat the Hamilton Beach Breakfast Sandwich Maker until the light turns green
2. Open the cover, the top ring, and the cooking plate
3. Butter all 12 slices of bread with the mayonnaise and butter
4. Beat the eggs in a small bowl and coat half of the bread slices with the egg mix
5. Put a slice of bread (buttered only) on the bottom ring of Hamilton Beach Breakfast Sandwich Maker
6. Top with the salad cress, lemon juice, cream cheese, and more salad
7. Lower the cooking plate and the top ring and add the egg coated bread
8. Close the cover and cook for 3 minutes
9. Repeat until all 12 slices are prepared
10. Serve.

Serving suggestion: serve with fruit juice

Preparation and Cooking Tips: Follow the instructions fastidiously

Nutritional value per serving: Calories: 156kcal, Fat: 15g, Carb: 21g, Proteins: 16g

Tomato Sandwich

It can get easier than the Tomato sandwich. Though simple, the meal is satisfying, flavourful, and most importantly, nutritious

Preparation time: 2 minutes

Cooking time: 4 minutes

Serves: 1

Ingredients To Use:

- 2 slices of gluten-free Bread
- 2 Thick Slices of Beefsteak Tomato
- 2 Tbsp of Eggless Vegan Mayo
- Salt and Pepper, as desired

Step-by-Step Directions to Cook It:

1. Preheat the Hamilton Beach Breakfast Sandwich Maker until the light turns green
2. Open the cover, the top ring, and the cooking plate
3. Butter the 2 slices of bread with the vegan mayo
4. Put a slice of bread on the bottom ring of Hamilton Beach Breakfast Sandwich Maker
5. Top with the tomato and sprinkle with pepper and salt.
6. Lower the cooking plate and the top ring, the other bread slice on the cooking plate
7. Close the cover and cook for 3 minutes

Serving suggestion: serve with fresh juice

Preparation and Cooking Tips: Follow the instructions fastidiously

Nutritional value per serving: Calories: 142kcal, Fat: 8g, Carb: 12g, Proteins: 11g

Waffle Sandwich

The pineapple twist in this sandwich recipe adds a nice exotic taste to your breakfast, and the egg is also loaded with protein.

Preparation time: 5 minutes

Cooking time: 12 minutes

Serves: 3

Ingredients To Use:

- 6 gluten-free waffle
- Sliced pineapple
- 6 slices of cheddar cheese

Step-by-Step Directions to Cook It:

1. Preheat the Hamilton Beach Breakfast Sandwich Maker until the light turns green
2. Open the cover, the top ring, and the cooking plate
3. Place one waffle in the bottom ring
4. Top with two thin slices of pineapple and cheddar cheese.
5. Place another waffle on the top ring of the sandwich maker.
6. Cook for 4 minutes, until the cheese completely melts.
7. Do the same to the other waffles.
8. Serve.

Serving suggestions: Best served warm

Preparation and Cooking Tips: Use a round waffle that'll fit the Hamilton Beach Breakfast Sandwich Maker

Nutritional value per serving: Calories: 210kcal, Fat: 12g, Carb: 20g, Proteins: 8g

Gluten-Free Pancake and Sausage Sandwich

Honey Glazed pancake and sausage sandwich is always a win-win combination for breakfast.

Preparation time: 5 minutes

Cooking time: 5 minutes

Serves: 1

Ingredients To Use:

- 2 pancakes
- 1 large egg
- 1 sausage, precooked
- Honey

Step-by-Step Directions to Cook It:

1. Turn on the Hamilton Beach Breakfast Sandwich Maker to preheat it for about 3 minutes.
2. Place one pancake on the bottom ring of the Hamilton Beach Breakfast Sandwich Maker
3. Top the pancake with sandwich patties
4. Lower the sandwich maker cooking plate and top ring. Pour beaten egg to the upper layer of the cooking plate and top with the pancake.
5. Cook for 5 minutes.
6. Remove lid and take out the sandwich.

Serving suggestions: Drizzle honey atop pancakes before serving.

Preparation and Cooking Tips: Precook sausage before making the sandwich and use a 4-inch frozen pancake.

Nutritional value per serving: Calories: 120kcal, Fat: 11g, Carb: 19g, Proteins: 8g

Blueberry Croissants

The sandwich is stuffed with tasty blueberries and is very easy to prepare.

Preparation time: 2 minutes

Cooking time: 3 minutes

Serves: 2

Ingredients To Use:

- 2 medium croissants
- 2 Tbsp. cream cheese
- ½ cup of blueberries, rinsed
- ¼ cup of honey

Step-by-Step Directions to Cook It:
1. Preheat the Hamilton Beach Breakfast Sandwich Maker
2. Slice the croissants into half and spread cheese on both slices
3. Place one croissant slice on the bottom ring of the sandwich maker.
4. Top with blueberries and drizzle honey over fruits.
5. Lower the cooking plate and the top ring
6. Place the other croissant on the upper plate. Cover
7. Cook for about 3 minutes.
8. Serve.

Serving suggestions: Serve while warm

Preparation and Cooking Tips: Don't cook for more than 5 minutes.

Nutritional value per serving: Calories: 285kcal, Fat: 15g, Carb: 23g, Proteins: 10g

Gluten-Free Muffin and Egg Sandwich

The recipe is packed with protein and also gluten-free. A great choice for a low-calorie sandwich breakfast.

Preparation time: 2 minutes

Cooking time: 5 minutes

Serves: 1

Ingredients To Use:

- 1 English Muffin, sliced vertically into half
- 1 slice of mozzarella cheese
- 2 large egg whites

Step-by-Step Directions to Cook It:

1. Preheat the Hamilton Beach Breakfast Sandwich Maker
2. Place one muffin slice on the bottom ring of the cooking plate.
3. Top with cheese.
4. Lower the cooking plate and top ring.
5. Add the egg to the plate and top with English muffin.
6. Cover the lid of the Sandwich maker and allow to cook for 5 minutes.
7. Use a plastic spatula to assemble the sandwich and transfer it to a serving plate

Serving suggestions: Drizzle maple syrup over the muffins

Preparation and Cooking Tips: Use thin slices of cheese to make the sandwich
Nutritional value per serving: Calories: 355kcal, Fat: 12g, Carb: 18g, Proteins:11 g

Cheese bagel and Buttered Egg

Butter adds flavor to the traditional fried egg sandwich, which makes the recipe low in calories.

Preparation time: 2 minutes

Cooking time: 5 minutes

Serves: 1

Ingredients To Use:

- 1 large egg
- 1 plain bagel, slice
- 1 pat of butter
- 1 slice of American cheese
- A pinch of salt
- Pepper, as desired

Step-by-Step Directions to Cook It:

1. Preheat the Hamilton Beach Breakfast Sandwich Maker
2. Place one slice of the bagel on the bottom ring of the sandwich maker
3. Top with cheese
4. Lower the cooking plate of the sandwich maker and drop the ring
5. Place butter on the plate until it melts.
6. Add the eggs and season to taste.
7. Top eggs with a bagel and cover lid.
8. Cook for about 5 minutes.
9. Serve.

Serving suggestions: Serve warm

Preparation and Cooking Tips: Increase the flavor of the sandwich by adding onion bagel.

Nutritional value per serving: Calories: 296kcal, Fat: 20g, Carb: 28g, Proteins: 11g

Gluten-free Egg Muffin and Bacon Sandwich

The recipe is delicious and can't go wrong when cooked with the Hamilton Beach Breakfast Sandwich Maker

Preparation time: 3 minutes

Cooking time: 5 minutes

Serves: 1

Ingredients To Use:

- 1 English Muffin, sliced vertically into half
- 2 slices of cooked bacon
- Salt and pepper to taste
- 1 slice of mozzarella cheese
- 2 large egg whites

Step-by-Step Directions to Cook It:

1. Preheat the Hamilton Beach Breakfast Sandwich Maker
2. Place one muffin slice on the bottom ring
3. Top muffin with cheese and bacon.
4. Lower the cooking plate and drop the rings.
5. Pour the egg on the plate and top with an English muffin.
6. Cover the lid of the sandwich maker and allow to cook for about 5 minutes.
7. Use a plastic spatula to assemble the sandwich and transfer it to a serving plate

Serving suggestions: Serve warm with orange slices

Preparation and Cooking Tips: Precook the bacon before adding it to the sandwich
Nutritional value per serving: Calories: 395kcal, Fat: 22g, Carb: 27g, Proteins: 21g

Ham and Omelet Sandwich

The recipe is made with simple ingredients that add a nice and delicious flavor to the sandwich.

Preparation time: 5 minutes

Cooking time: 5 minutes

Serves:

Ingredients To Use:

- 4 Gluten-free Bagel, sliced into halves
- 1 cup of ham, chopped
- 3 Tbsp of gluten-free milk
- 1 cup of cheese, shredded
- Salt and pepper to taste

Step-by-Step Directions to Cook It:
1. Preheat the Hamilton Beach Breakfast Sandwich Maker
2. Mix egg, milk, salt, and pepper in a medium-sized bowl.
3. Add chopped ham to the whisked egg.
4. Place one bagel slice on the bottom ring of the appliance
5. Top bagel slice with one-quarter of the cheese
6. Lower the cooking plate and drop the ring.
7. Pour in the egg mixture and top with another slice of bagel.
8. Cook for 5 minutes.
9. Repeat the procedure for the rest of the bagels.

Serving suggestions: Serve immediately

Preparation and Cooking Tips: Add dried basil to boost the taste of the sandwich
Nutritional value per serving: Calories: 427kcal, Fat: 27g, Carb: 23g, Proteins: 21g

Turkey Bacon and Gluten-Free Muffins

Turkey bacon is a good choice for a low-fat sandwich breakfast on a cold holiday morning.

Preparation time: 2 minutes

Cooking time: 5 minutes

Serves:

Ingredients To Use:

- 1 gluten-free muffin, sliced
- 2 slices of cooked turkey bacon
- 1 slice of mozzarella cheese
- 2 large eggs

Step-by-Step Directions to Cook It:
1. Preheat the Hamilton Beach Breakfast Sandwich Maker
2. Place one muffin slice on the bottom ring of the appliance
3. Top muffin with cheese and bacon.
4. Lower the cooking plate and drop the rings.
5. Pour the egg on the plate and top with an English muffin.
6. Cover the lid of the sandwich maker and allow to cook for about 5 minutes.
7. Use a plastic spatula to assemble the sandwich and transfer it to a serving plate

Serving suggestions: Serve warm

Preparation and Cooking Tips: Use cooked turkey bacon to prepare the sandwich
Nutritional value per serving: Calories: 295kcal, Fat: 15g, Carb: 18g, Proteins: 22g

Bacon and Waffle Sandwich

A gluten-free waffle sandwich with bacon patty and a slice of cheese is a healthy breakfast choice that you wouldn't love to miss.

Preparation time: 3 minutes

Cooking time: 5 minutes

Serves:

Ingredients To Use:

- 1 cooked bacon, made into patties
- 1 large egg
- 2 frozen waffles
- 1 oz. cheddar cheese

Step-by-Step Directions to Cook It:

1. Preheat the Hamilton Beach Breakfast Sandwich Maker
2. Place one frozen waffle slice on the bottom ring
3. Top waffle with bacon and cheese.
4. Lower the cooking plate and drop the rings.
5. Beat the egg in a medium bowl and pour it on the upper cooking plate.
6. Top with another slice of frozen waffles
7. Cover the lid of the sandwich maker and allow to cook for about 5 minutes.
8. Use a plastic spatula to assemble the sandwich and transfer it to a serving plate

Serving suggestions: Serve warm

Preparation and Cooking Tips: Use frozen waffles to avoid making soggy sandwich.
Nutritional value per serving: Calories: 305kcal, Fat: 18g, Carb: 20g, Proteins: 19g

Steak Stuffed Pancake Sandwich

The steak sandwich recipe is a good way to use leftover steaks from dinner to make protein loaded breakfast.

Preparation time: 2 minutes

Cooking time: 4 minutes

Serves: 1

Ingredients To Use:

- 1 Tsp. grainy mustard
- 2 frozen gluten-free pancake
- 1 large egg
- 2 oz. cooked steak, thinly sliced

Step-by-Step Directions to Cook It:

1. Preheat the Hamilton Beach Breakfast Sandwich Maker
2. Place one frozen pancake slice on the bottom ring and spread mustard over it.
3. Top with steak slices.
4. Lower the cooking plate and drop the rings.
5. Beat the egg in a medium bowl and pour it on the upper cooking plate.
6. Top with another slice of frozen waffles
7. Cover the lid of the sandwich maker and allow to cook for about 5 minutes.
8. Use a plastic spatula to assemble the sandwich and transfer it to a serving plate

Serving suggestions: Serve with avocado slices

Preparation and Cooking Tips: Add blue cheese to the steak after 3 minutes of cooking time.

Nutritional value per serving: Calories: 143kcal, Fat: 8g, Carb: 14g, Proteins: 9g

Chapter 8: Snacks and Desserts

Cookie Nutella stack

This delicious gooey cookie dessert is lip-smacking and can be easily prepared with the sandwich maker.

Preparation time: 3 minutes

Cooking time: 5 minutes

Serves: 1

Ingredients To Use:

- 2 Tbsp of chocolate spread, Nutella
- 2 large chocolate cookies, store-bought
- ¼ cup of wild raspberries

Step-by-Step Directions to Cook It:

1. Preheat the Hamilton Beach Breakfast Sandwich Maker
2. Spread the Nutella atop the cookies.
3. Place cookies on the bottom ring of the sandwich maker with the chocolate side facing up.
4. Top with ½ portion of the raspberries
5. Lower the cooking plate and drop the rings.
6. Add the rest of the raspberries and top with cookies, with the chocolate spread side facing down.
7. Cook for 4 minutes.

Serving suggestions: Allow to cool before serving

Preparation and Cooking Tips: Use fresh berries for best results

Nutritional value per serving: Calories: 152kcal, Fat: 11g, Carb: 15g, Proteins: 5g

Marshmallows Toast

This chocolate and marshmallow camping inspired combo recipe is something you'll never want to miss out on during a trip.

Preparation time: 3 minutes

Cooking time: 3 minutes

Serves: 1

Ingredients To Use:

- 1 pat of butter
- 1 oz. milk chocolate bars, sliced
- 2 marshmallows
- 2 slices of raisin bread, cut into round fits

Step-by-Step Directions to Cook It:

1. Coat the bottom ring with butter and then preheat the Hamilton Beach Breakfast Sandwich Maker
2. Place bread on the bottom ring and top with chocolate bar slices.
3. Coat the top compartment of the cooking plate with butter and add marshmallows.
4. Top with the second slice of bread.
5. Cook for 3 minutes.

Serving suggestions: Serve warm

Preparation and Cooking Tips: Butter cooking plate to prevent sticking

Nutritional value per serving: Calories: 855kcal, Fat: 32g, Carb: 122g, Proteins: 13g

Strawberry Stuffed Biscuit Sandwich

This recipe is another twist to the traditional biscuit sandwich. It's juicy and perfect for a hot afternoon.

Preparation time: 3 minutes

Cooking time: 3 minutes

Serves: 1

Ingredients To Use:

- ¼ Tsp. sugar
- 2 large biscuits, store-bought
- ¼ cup of halved strawberries
- ¼ cup of whipped cream

Step-by-Step Directions to Cook It:
1. Preheat the Hamilton Beach Breakfast Sandwich Maker
2. Add biscuit to the bottom ring of the sandwich maker.
3. Drop the cooking plate and top ring
4. Arrange strawberries over the cooking plate and sprinkle in sugar
5. Top strawberries with a biscuit if desired.
6. Cook for 3 minutes.

Serving suggestions: Serve with whipped cream

Preparation and Cooking Tips: Use powdered sugar to prepare the sandwich

Nutritional value per serving: Calories: 391kcal, Fat: 16g, Carb: 51g, Proteins: 12g

Fig Flavoured Croissant

Figs add a fresh flavor to croissants, and the best part is that they're easily accessible with little cost.

Preparation time: 3 minutes

Cooking time: 3 minutes

Serves: 1

Ingredients To Use:

- 1 croissant, halved and cut into a round fit
- 2 Tsp. maple syrup
- 1 oz. goat cheese
- 2 fresh figs, quartered

Step-by-Step Directions to Cook It:

1. Preheat the Hamilton Beach Breakfast Sandwich Maker
2. Place one slice of croissant on the bottom ring of the sandwich maker.
3. Top with goat cheese and drizzle in maple syrup.
4. Lower the cooking plate and drop the rings.
5. Add the fresh figs and top with a croissant.
6. Cook for about 5 minutes and assemble the sandwich.

Serving suggestions: Drizzle in more honey syrup atop the sandwich

Preparation and Cooking Tips: Use fresh figs to add a robust flavor.

Nutritional value per serving: Calories: 325kcal, Fat: 19g, Carb: 25g, Proteins: 8g

Pie Filled Donut Sandwich

This recipe is a pie version of a donut sandwich that's irresistible to pie loving fans. It's also easy to make.

Preparation time: 3 minutes

Cooking time: 4 minutes

Serves: 1

Ingredients To Use:

- 1 cinnamon-sugar cake donut, cut into half
- 1 Tbsp. caramel sauce
- ¼ cup of apple filling

Step-by-Step Directions to Cook It:

1. Preheat the Hamilton Beach Breakfast Sandwich Maker
2. Place donut on the bottom ring of the sandwich maker.
3. Top with apple filling.
4. Lower the cooking plate and drop the rings.
5. Place the other slice of the donut atop the cooking plate, cut side facing down.
6. Cook for 4 minutes.
7. Drizzle caramel sauce atop the sandwich

Serving suggestions: Serve with a dollop of vanilla ice cream

Preparation and Cooking Tips: Preheat sandwich maker before use

Nutritional value per serving: Calories: 315kcal, Fat: 20g, Carb: 25g, Proteins: 15g

Chocolate and Sourdough Sandwich

This chocolate sandwich combo recipe is creamy, yummy, and also has a blend of nuts and fruits.

Preparation time: 3 minutes

Cooking time: 4 minutes

Serves:

Ingredients To Use:

- 1 Tbsp. chocolate- hazelnut spread, nutella
- 2 Tbsp. soft brie cheese, cut into a round fit
- ½ cup of fresh raspberries

Step-by-Step Directions to Cook It:

1. Preheat the Hamilton Beach Breakfast Sandwich Maker
2. Spread the Nutella on the cut side of the bread
3. Place bread on the bottom ring of the sandwich maker.
4. Add brie to the Nutella spread bread.
5. Lower the cooking plate and drop the rings.
6. Add the raspberries and top with bread.
7. Cook for 4 minutes.

Serving suggestions: Serve while warm with whipped cream

Preparation and Cooking Tips: Use fresh raspberries

Nutritional value per serving: Calories: 340kcal, Fat: 18g, Carb: 28g, Proteins: 10g

White chocolate and Banana Sandwich

Chocolate fans will love this sandwich fruit twist, which combines butter, chocolate, and banana to make a yummy dessert.

Preparation time: 3 minutes

Cooking time: 4 minutes

Serves: 1

Ingredients To Use:

- 1 ripe banana, thinly sliced
- 1 Tsp. almond butter
- 1 large cookie, store-bought or homemade
- 1 Tbsp. white chocolate, melted

Step-by-Step Directions to Cook It:

1. Preheat the Hamilton Beach Breakfast Sandwich Maker
2. Spread the almond butter atop the cookie
3. Place cookies on the bottom ring of the sandwich maker with the buttered side facing up.
4. Add half portion of bananas atop it.
5. Lower the cooking plate and drop the rings.
6. Add the remaining portion of banana and drizzle chocolate atop it.
7. Cook for 4 minutes.

Serving suggestions: Serve with ice cream

Preparation and Cooking Tips: Use ripe bananas to prepare sandwich
Nutritional value per serving: Calories: 225kcal, Fat: 19g, Carb: 20g, Proteins: 5g

Banana Stuffed Sandwich

Kids love peanuts, and this recipe is a perfect choice to make them a healthy muffin flavored peanut butter sandwich.

Preparation time: 2 minutes

Cooking time: 4 minutes

Serves: 1

Ingredients To Use:

- 1 English muffin, halved
- 1 ripe banana, thinly sliced
- 2 Tsp. peanut butter

Step-by-Step Directions to Cook It:

1. Preheat the Hamilton Beach Breakfast Sandwich Maker
2. Spread the peanut butter on the cut side of the muffin
3. Place muffins on the bottom ring of the sandwich maker with the buttered side facing up.
4. Add half portion of the banana atop it.
5. Lower the cooking plate and drop the rings.
6. Add the remaining portion of the banana and top with muffins.
7. Cook for 4 minutes.

Serving suggestions: Serve warm

Preparation and Cooking Tips: Use ripe bananas to prepare the sandwich.

Nutritional value per serving: Calories: 198kcal, Fat: 18g, Carb: 26g, Proteins: 9g

Creamy Waffles

This recipe is creamy and melts right in the mouth. It's perfect for a holiday snack and also easy to make.

Preparation time: 5 minutes

Cooking time: 5 minutes

Serves: 1

Ingredients To Use:

- 1 Tbsp. powdered sugar
- 2 frozen waffles, leftovers
- 1/8 Tsp. ground cinnamon
- 1 Tbsp. heavy cream
- 1 large egg
- ¼ Tsp. vanilla extract

Step-by-Step Directions to Cook It:

1. Preheat the Hamilton Beach Breakfast Sandwich Maker
2. In a medium-sized bowl, mix the cream, egg, vanilla, cinnamon, and sugar until soft beats are formed.
3. Place waffles on the bottom ring of the sandwich maker.
4. Lower the cooking plate and drop the rings.
5. Pour the egg mixture on the upper part of the cooking plate and topple with waffle.
6. Cook for 5 minutes.

Serving suggestions: Serve with fruits.

Preparation and Cooking Tips: Use frozen waffles

Nutritional value per serving: Calories: 345kcal, Fat: 27g, Carb: 30g, Proteins: 10g

Peach and Biscuit Sandwich

Cheese adds an extra creaminess to this recipe. It also blends well with the ripe peach and biscuit in this recipe.

Preparation time: 2 minutes

Cooking time: 4 minutes

Serves:

Ingredients To Use:

- 1 homemade biscuit, sliced
- 1 Tbsp. maple syrup
- 1 Tbsp. powdered sugar (optional)
- 1 yellow peach, peeled and sliced.

Step-by-Step Directions to Cook It:

1. Preheat the Hamilton Beach Breakfast Sandwich Maker
2. Place biscuit on the bottom ring of the sandwich maker and top with half portion of cheese.
3. Drizzle syrup atop cheese.
4. Lower the cooking plate and drop the rings.
5. Add the remaining portion of cheese and top with cookie
6. Cook for 4 minutes.

Serving suggestions: Serve with whipped cream

Preparation and Cooking Tips: Mix peach and sugar in a bowl and sit for 3 minutes before use.

Nutritional value per serving: Calories: 110kcal, Fat: 12g, Carb: 19g, Proteins: 3g

Chapter 9: Keto Breakfast Sandwiches

Eggs with Parmesan and Veggie Sandwich

This is an amazing recipe because it is for both vegetarian and non-vegetarian. It is an incredible breakfast recipe

Preparation time: 5 minutes

 Cooking time: 5 minutes

Serves: 1

Ingredients To Use:

- 1 egg
- 1 cup diced zucchini
- Pepper and salt
- Cinnamon bread slices
- 1/8 cup of diced mushrooms
- 1 diced small red pepper
- 1/8 cup of parmesan cheese, grated
- 1 small chopped yellow onion

Step-by-Step Directions to Cook It:

1. Preheat the Hamilton Beach Breakfast Sandwich Maker until the light turns green
2. Mix mushroom, zucchini, peppers, and onion in a bowl
3. Whisk egg and sprinkle pepper and salt
4. Add the two mixtures together
5. Open the cover, the top ring, and the cooking plate
6. Put a slice of cinnamon bread on the bottom ring of Hamilton Beach Breakfast Sandwich Maker
7. Lower the cooking plate and the top ring
8. Put egg mix in the cooking plate. Close the cover and cook for 5 minutes
9. Rotate the cooking plate handle clockwise until it stops, serve immediately

Serving suggestion: serve with coffee

Preparation and Cooking Tips: dice the zucchini, mushroom, and red pepper. Chop the onion

Nutritional value per serving: Calories: 216kcal, Fat: 15g, Carb: 6g, Proteins: 20g

Butter Almond Muffin

This recipe has a mouth-watering taste. It is a delightful and flavourful recipe

Preparation time: 10 minutes

Cooking time: 10 minutes

Serves: 2

Ingredients To Use:

- ½ cup of almond flour
- 1/8 cup of almond butter
- Green veggie
- Muffin split
- 1/8 cup of powdered erythritol
- 1/8 cup of unsweetened almond milk
- 1 tsp of baking powder
- 1 big egg
- 1/8 tsp of salt

Step-by-Step Directions to Cook It:

1. Preheat the Hamilton Beach Breakfast Sandwich Maker until the light turns green
2. Mix baking powder, almond flour, and erythritol in a bowl
3. Mix egg, almond milk, and almond butter in another bowl
4. Add the 2 mixtures together in a bowl
5. Open the cover, the top ring, and the cooking plate
6. Put muffin split on the bottom ring of Hamilton Beach Breakfast Sandwich Maker
7. Top with a green veggie
8. Lower the cooking plate and the top ring, put egg mix in the cooking plate, cover with another muffin mix
9. Close the cover and cook for 10 minutes
10. Rotate the cooking plate handle clockwise until it stops, serve immediately

Serving suggestion: serve with tea

Preparation and Cooking Tips: unsweetened almond milk should be used

Nutritional value per serving: Calories: 136kcal, Fat: 12g, Carb: 5g, Proteins: 7g

Western Omelet Classic

Classic omelet depicts its name because it is exquisite and extra-ordinary. Enjoy the amazing breakfast

Preparation time: 5 minutes

Cooking time: 5 minutes

Serves: 1

Ingredients To Use:

- 2 tsp of coconut oil
- ¼ cup of diced ham
- 3 large eggs, whisked
- ¼ cup of diced green pepper
- 1 tbsp of heavy cream
- ¼ cup of diced yellow onion
- Bread slices
- Pepper and salt

Step-by-Step Directions to Cook It:

1. Preheat the Hamilton Beach Breakfast Sandwich Maker until the light turns green
2. Mix coconut oil, green pepper, ham, and onion in a bowl
3. Mix eggs, pepper, heavy cream, and salt in another bowl
4. Open the cover, the top ring, and the cooking plate
5. Put bread slice on the bottom ring of Hamilton Beach Breakfast Sandwich Maker
6. Top with the onion mix
7. Lower the cooking plate and the top ring, put egg mix in the cooking plate, cover with another slice of bread
8. Close the cover and cook for 6 minutes
9. Rotate the cooking plate handle clockwise until it stops, serve immediately

Serving suggestion: serve with sauce

Preparation and Cooking Tips: dice the green pepper and the yellow onion

Nutritional value per serving: Calories: 416kcal, Fat: 33g, Carb: 7g, Proteins: 26g

Cinnamon Sandwich

This is an exceptional way of making a sandwich. Using different ingredients to explore the sandwich world. It is a unique recipe

Preparation time: 5 minutes

Cooking time: 5 minutes

Serves: 2

Ingredients To Use:

- ½ cup of coconut milk
- ½ tsp of vanilla extract
- 1/8 cup of coconut oil
- Cinnamon bread slices
- Liquid stevia extract
- 3 big eggs
- ¼ tsp of ground cinnamon
- 1 scoop of protein powder egg white
- Ground nutmeg

Step-by-Step Directions to Cook It:

1. Preheat the Hamilton Beach Breakfast Sandwich Maker until the light turns green
2. Mix eggs, coconut milk, and coconut oil in a bowl whisk well
3. Add protein powder, vanilla extract, cinnamon, nutmeg, and stevia extract, whisk well
4. Open the cover, the top ring, and the cooking plate
5. Put cinnamon bread on the bottom ring of Hamilton Beach Breakfast Sandwich Maker
6. Lower the cooking plate and the top ring, put egg mix in the cooking plate, cover with another cinnamon bread
7. Close the cover and cook for 10 minutes
8. Rotate the cooking plate handle clockwise until it stops, serve immediately

Serving suggestion: serve with cream

Preparation and Cooking Tips: use grounded cinnamon

Nutritional value per serving: Calories: 441kcal, Fat: 39g, Carb: 6g, Proteins: 23g

Pepper Jack, Ham with Egg Sandwich

A combination of ham, pepper jack cheese, and egg makes an amazing sandwich.

Preparation time: 5 minutes

Cooking time: 5 minutes

Serves: 2

Ingredients To Use:

- 2 big eggs
- Hoagie buns split
- ¼ cup of pepper jack cheese, shredded
- Pepper and salt
- 1 cup of diced ham

Step-by-Step Directions to Cook It:

1. Preheat the Hamilton Beach Breakfast Sandwich Maker until the light turns green
2. Mix eggs, ham, pepper, cheese, and salt in a bowl
3. Open the cover, the top ring, and the cooking plate
4. Put hoagie buns on the bottom ring of Hamilton Beach Breakfast Sandwich Maker
5. Lower the cooking plate and the top ring, put the egg mixture in the cooking plate, cover with a hoagie bun
6. Close the cover and cook for 5 minutes
7. Rotate the cooking plate handle clockwise until it stops, serve immediately

Serving suggestion: serve with cream cheese

Preparation and Cooking Tips: dice the ham

Nutritional value per serving: Calories: 236kcal, Fat: 16g, Carb: 3g, Proteins: 22g

Crispy Cardamon Sandwich

The crispy waffle is a delicious recipe with a finger-licking taste. It is easy and fast to make.

Preparation time: 5 minutes

Cooking time: 5 minutes

Serves: 2

Ingredients To Use:

- 2 big eggs, whites and yolks, separated
- ¼ tsp of ground cinnamon
- 1 ½ tbsp. of coconut flour
- ½ tsp of vanilla extract
- 1 ½ tbsp. of powdered
- 1/8 tsp of ground ginger
- erythritol
- Ground cardamom
- Slices of soft bread
- 1 ½ tbsp. of unsweetened almond milk
- 1 tsp of baking powder
- Ground cloves
- 1 ½ tbsp. of melted coconut oil

Step-by-Step Directions to Cook It:

1. Preheat the Hamilton Beach Breakfast Sandwich Maker until the light turns green
2. Whisk egg white and egg yolk in 2 separate bowls
3. Mix egg yolk with baking powder, cardamom, coconut flour, cloves, vanilla, cinnamon, and erythritol in a bowl.
4. Add almond milk and melted coconut oil
5. Transfer the mixture to egg white bowl and whisk well
6. Open the cover, the top ring, and the cooking plate
7. Put soft bread slices on the bottom ring of Hamilton Beach Breakfast Sandwich Maker
8. Lower the cooking plate and the top ring, put egg mix in the cooking plate, cover with soft bread slice. Close the cover and cook for 5 minutes
9. Rotate the cooking plate handle clockwise until it stops, serve immediately

Serving suggestion: serve with coffee

Preparation and Cooking Tips: separate the egg yolk from the egg white

Nutritional value per serving: Calories: 216kcal, Fat: 18g, Carb: 9g, Proteins: 9g

Scramble Egg Broccoli Kale

A combination of broccoli and kale makes a nutritional scramble egg; It makes a delightful recipe.

Preparation time: 5 minutes

Cooking time: 5 minutes

Serves: 1

Ingredients To Use:

- 2 big eggs
- 1 tsp of coconut oil
- 2 tbsp of grated parmesan cheese
- 1 tbsp of heavy cream
- 1 cup of fresh chopped kale
- Slices of Italian bread
- Salt and pepper
- ¼ cup of broccoli florets, frozen

Step-by-Step Directions to Cook It:

1. Preheat the Hamilton Beach Breakfast Sandwich Maker until the light turns green
2. Mix eggs with pepper, heavy cream, and salt. Add broccoli, coconut oil, and kale to it
3. Open the cover, the top ring, and the cooking plate
4. Put a slice of Italian bread on the bottom ring of Hamilton Beach Breakfast Sandwich Maker
5. Lower the cooking plate and the top ring, put the egg mix in the cooking plate, add a slice of bread
6. Close the cover and cook for 5 minutes
7. Rotate the cooking plate handle clockwise until it stops, serve immediately

Serving suggestion: serve with cheese

Preparation and Cooking Tips: grate the cheese, chop the kale and thaw the broccoli

Nutritional value per serving: Calories: 316kcal, Fat: 24g, Carb: 11g, Proteins: 20g

Egg Muffin Cheese Sandwich

Egg muffin with cheese is a soft recipe. It also melts easily in the mouth. Try this procedure and enjoy the muffin

Preparation time: 5 minutes

Cooking time: 5 minutes

Serves: 1

Ingredients To Use:

- 2 slices of bread
- ½ tsp of butter
- Pepper and salt
- 1 tsp of diced yellow onion
- 1 tsp of shredded cheddar cheese
- 1 big egg
- 1 tbsp of grated parmesan cheese
- 1 tsp of canned coconut milk
- 1 tsp of sliced green onion
- 1 tbsp of Swiss cheese, shredded

Step-by-Step Directions to Cook It:

1. Preheat the Hamilton Beach Breakfast Sandwich Maker until the light turns green
2. Mix coconut milk, pepper, eggs, green onion, coconut milk, salt, and onion in a bowl
3. Open the cover, the top ring, and the cooking plate
4. Put a slice of bread on the bottom ring of Hamilton Beach Breakfast Sandwich Maker
5. Top with cheese
6. Lower the cooking plate and the top ring, put egg mix in the cooking plate, cover with bread slice
7. Close the cover and cook for 5 minutes
8. Rotate the cooking plate handle clockwise until it stops, serve immediately

Serving suggestion: serve with cream

Preparation and Cooking Tips: dice the onion and grate the cheese

Nutritional value per serving: Calories: 151kcal, Fat: 12g, Carb: 3g, Proteins: 11g

Almond Cinnamon Porridge Sandwich

This is a special meal; it is a lot of nutritional benefits. This is a good breakfast for a long day.

Preparation time: 5 minutes

 Cooking time: 5 minutes

Serves: 1

Ingredients To Use:

- Bread slices
- 1 tbsp of butter
- 1 tbsp of almond butter
- 1 tbsp of coconut flour
- ¼ cup of canned coconut milk
- 1 big egg
- Salt
- ⅛ tsp of ground cinnamon

Step-by-Step Directions to Cook It:
1. Preheat the Hamilton Beach Breakfast Sandwich Maker until the light turns green
2. Mix egg, butter, salt, cinnamon, and coconut flour in a bowl, add coconut milk
3. Open the cover, the top ring, and the cooking plate
4. Put a slice of bread on the bottom ring of Hamilton Beach Breakfast Sandwich Maker
5. Top with cheese
6. Lower the cooking plate and the top ring, put egg mix in the cooking plate, cover with another slice of bread
7. Close the cover and cook for 5 minutes
8. Rotate the cooking plate handle clockwise until it stops, serve immediately

Serving suggestion: serve with cheese

Preparation and Cooking Tips: whisk the egg well

Nutritional value per serving: Calories: 471kcal, Fat: 43g, Carb: 16g, Proteins: 14g

Mushroom Bacon with Swiss Omelette

This is an amazing omelette with a sweet taste. It has a great last long flavor.

Preparation time: 5 minutes

 Cooking time: 5 minutes

Serves: 1

Ingredients To Use:

- ¼ cup of diced mushrooms
- 3 big eggs
- 2 slices of uncooked bacon
- Slices of bread
- 1 tbsp of heavy cream
- ¼ cup of Swiss cheese, shredded
- Pepper and salt

Step-by-Step Directions to Cook It:

1. Preheat the Hamilton Beach Breakfast Sandwich Maker until the light turns green
2. Mix egg, salt, heavy cream, and pepper in a bowl
3. Open the cover, the top ring, and the cooking plate
4. Put a slice of bread on the bottom ring of Hamilton Beach Breakfast Sandwich Maker
5. Top with a bacon slice, mushroom
6. Lower the cooking plate and the top ring, put egg mix in the cooking plate, cover with another slice of bread
7. Close the cover and cook for 5 minutes
8. Rotate the cooking plate handle clockwise until it stops, serve immediately

Serving suggestion: serve with cream

Preparation and Cooking Tips: slice the bacon and dice the mushroom

Nutritional value per serving: Calories: 476kcal, Fat: 37g, Carb: 5g, Proteins: 35g

Chapter 10: Paleo Breakfast Sandwiches

Mushroom Onion with Tomato Scrambled Eggs Sandwich

This is a unique way of making scrambled eggs. It is less stressful and easy to make.

Preparation time: 5 minutes

Cooking time: 5 minutes

Serves: 2

Ingredients To Use:

- 4 big eggs
- ½ cup of chopped tomatoes
- 3 chopped spring onions
- 1 cup of cubed ham
- ½ cup of chopped mushrooms
- Soft bread slices

Step-by-Step Directions to Cook It:

1. Preheat the Hamilton Beach Breakfast Sandwich Maker until the light turns green
2. Mix onion, mushrooms, ham, and tomatoes in a bowl
3. Whisk eggs in another bowl
4. Open the cover, the top ring, and the cooking plate
5. Put a slice of soft bread on the bottom ring of Hamilton Beach Breakfast Sandwich Maker
6. Lower the cooking plate and the top ring, put egg and tomato mix in the cooking plate, cover with another slice of soft bread
7. Close the cover and cook for 5 minutes
8. Rotate the cooking plate handle clockwise until it stops, serve immediately

Serving suggestion: serve with juice

Preparation and Cooking Tips: chop the tomatoes and mushroom, cut the ham into cubes

Nutritional value per serving: Calories: 270kcal, Fat: 21g, Carb: 10g, Proteins: 13g

Prosciutto Sandwich

This is an incredible sandwich. It is fluffy and soft. This is a good recipe to eat for breakfast.

Preparation time: 5 minutes

 Cooking time: 5 minutes

Serves: 1

Ingredients To Use:

- 2 slices of prosciutto
- Pepper
- 1 egg

Step-by-Step Directions to Cook It:
1. Preheat the Hamilton Beach Breakfast Sandwich Maker until the light turns green
2. Open the cover, the top ring, and the cooking plate
3. Mix pepper and egg in a bowl, whisk well
4. Put a slice of prosciutto on the bottom ring of Hamilton Beach Breakfast Sandwich Maker
5. Lower the cooking plate and the top ring, put egg mix in the cooking plate, cover with another slice of soft bread
6. Close the cover and cook for 5 minutes
7. Rotate the cooking plate handle clockwise until it stops, serve immediately

Serving suggestion: serve with cheese

Preparation and Cooking Tips: add the pepper to taste

Nutritional value per serving: Calories: 895kcal, Fat: 47g, Carb: 65g, Proteins: 51g

Avocado and Shrimp Omelette Sandwich

This sandwich is a unique sandwich with nutritional ingredients. It brightens the day.

Preparation time: 5 minutes

Cooking time: 10 minutes

Serves: 2

Ingredients To Use:

- 5 eggs
- ½ lb of deveined shrimp
- 1 avocado
- Bread slices
- 1 diced plum tomato
- 1 tsp of coconut oil

Step-by-Step Directions to Cook It:
1. Preheat the Hamilton Beach Breakfast Sandwich Maker until the light turns green
2. Open the cover, the top ring, and the cooking plate
3. Put a slice of bread on the bottom ring of Hamilton Beach Breakfast Sandwich Maker
4. Top with avocado, tomato, and shrimp
5. Lower the cooking plate and the top ring, break eggs into the cooking plate, cover with another slice of bread
6. Close the cover and cook for 8 minutes
7. Rotate the cooking plate handle clockwise until it stops, serve immediately

Serving suggestion: serve with coconut oil

Preparation and Cooking Tips: dice the avocado, peel and devein the shrimps

Nutritional value per serving: Calories: 385kcal, Fat: 27g, Carb: 12g, Proteins: 29g

Pumpkin Paleo Sandwich

This sandwich is an incredible and great recipe. It has the best taste.

Preparation time: 5 minutes

Cooking time: 10 minutes

Serves: 2

Ingredients To Use:

- ½ cup of dried apricots
- 1/8 tsp of sea salt
- 1 cup of walnuts
- ½ tbsp. of vanilla extract
- 1 organic egg

Step-by-Step Directions to Cook It:

1. Preheat the Hamilton Beach Breakfast Sandwich Maker until the light turns green
2. Open the cover, the top ring, and the cooking plate
3. Mix walnut, apricot, vanilla extract, and sea salt
4. Put half of the walnut mix on the bottom ring of Hamilton Beach Breakfast Sandwich Maker
5. Lower the cooking plate and the top ring, break eggs into the cooking plate, cover with the remaining half walnut mix
6. Close the cover and cook for 10 minutes
7. Rotate the cooking plate handle clockwise until it stops, serve immediately

Serving suggestion: serve with juice

Preparation and Cooking Tips: any extract can be used

Nutritional value per serving: Calories: 186kcal, Fat: 13g, Carb: 14g, Proteins: 8g

Egg and Eggplants sandwich

This is a pleasant sandwich. It is a nutritious and amazing recipe that can be taken at any time of the day

Preparation time: 5 minutes

Cooking time: 5 minutes

Serves: 2

Ingredients To Use:

- Pepper and salt
- 2 eggplants, sliced
- Italian bread slices
- Coconut oil
- 3 medium eggs

Step-by-Step Directions to Cook It:

1. Preheat the Hamilton Beach Breakfast Sandwich Maker until the light turns green
2. Open the cover, the top ring, and the cooking plate
3. Mix pepper, eggs, and salt in a bowl.
4. Put a slice of bread on the bottom ring of Hamilton Beach Breakfast Sandwich Maker
5. Top with eggplant
6. Lower the cooking plate and the top ring, egg mix the cooking plate, cover with another bread slice
7. Close the cover and cook for 5 minutes
8. Rotate the cooking plate handle clockwise until it stops, serve immediately

Serving suggestion: serve with coconut oil

Preparation and Cooking Tips: slice the eggplants to disc

Nutritional value per serving: Calories: 21kcal, Fat: 3g, Carb: 6g, Proteins: 2g

Veggie and Sausage Breakfast Sandwich

Sausage roll with a veggie makes an energizing sandwich. It is a good breakfast recipe

Preparation time: 5 minutes

Cooking time: 10 minutes

Serves: 2

Ingredients To Use:

- ½ onion, chopped
- 2 sausage rolls, split
- 3 cups of spinach
- 1 tsp of coconut oil
- ½ lb of sausage

Step-by-Step Directions to Cook It:

1. Preheat the Hamilton Beach Breakfast Sandwich Maker until the light turns green
2. Open the cover, the top ring, and the cooking plate
3. Put a split of a sausage roll on the bottom ring of Hamilton Beach Breakfast Sandwich Maker
4. Top with spinach
5. Lower the cooking plate and the top ring, put the sausage on the cooking plate, cover with another sausage roll split
6. Close the cover and cook for 10 minutes
7. Rotate the cooking plate handle clockwise until it stops, serve immediately

Serving suggestion: serve with coconut oil

Preparation and Cooking Tips: roughly chop the onion

Nutritional value per serving: Calories: 332kcal, Fat: 16g, Carb: 28g, Proteins: 27g

Eggs with Pork Steak Sandwich

This sandwich is power-packed and delivers the required energy to get you through a busy day.

Preparation time: 5 minutes

Cooking time: 5 minutes

Serves: 2

Ingredients To Use:

- ½ lb of pre-cooked and sliced pork steak
- 1 chopped red bell pepper
- ¼ onion, diced
- 2 eggs
- Wheat bread
- 4 mushrooms, chopped

Step-by-Step Directions to Cook It:

1. Preheat the Hamilton Beach Breakfast Sandwich Maker until the light turns green
2. Open the cover, the top ring, and the cooking plate
3. Put a slice of wheat bread on the bottom ring of Hamilton Beach Breakfast Sandwich Maker
4. Top with pork slice, red bell pepper, mushroom, and onion
5. Lower the cooking plate and the top ring
6. Put eggs on the cooking plate, cover with wheat bread slice
7. Close the cover and cook for 5 minutes
8. Rotate the cooking plate handle clockwise until it stops, serve immediately

Serving suggestion: serve with butter

Preparation and Cooking Tips: chop the bell pepper and the mushroom

Nutritional value per serving: Calories: 167kcal, Fat: 12g, Carb: 4g, Proteins: 15g

Banana Egg Sandwich

The banana egg sandwich is crispy and delicious. Follow the procedure below and have a great sandwich

Preparation time: 5 minutes

Cooking time: 10 minutes

Serves: 2

Ingredients To Use:

- ¼ cup of walnuts
- 1 handful of berries, fresh
- ¼ tsp. of ground ginger
- ½ cup of unsweetened almond milk
- ¼ cup of pecans
- 1 Tbsp of almond butter
- 2 Tbsp of ground flax seed
- 1 mashed banana
- 2 muffin split
- 1 tsp. of ground cinnamon, mashed
- 3 eggs

Step-by-Step Directions to Cook It:

1. Blend the pecans, flaxseed, and walnut in a blender and set aside
2. Preheat the Hamilton Beach Breakfast Sandwich Maker until the light turns green
3. Open the cover, the top ring, and the cooking plate
4. Mix egg and almond milk
5. Put a muffin split, buttered up on the bottom ring of Hamilton Beach Breakfast Sandwich Maker
6. Top with nut mix, mashed banana, ginger, and cinnamon
7. Lower the cooking plate and the top ring
8. Put eggs mix the cooking plate, cover with muffin split
9. Close the cover and cook for 5 minutes
10. Rotate the cooking plate handle clockwise until it stops, serve immediately

Serving suggestion: serve with berries

Preparation and Cooking Tips: mash the banana

Nutritional value per serving: Calories: 360kcal, Fat: 17g, Carb: 33g, Proteins: 20g

Mushroom Omelette Sandwich

This is a yummy sandwich. It has a nourishing taste and sweet savor

Preparation time: 5 minutes

Cooking time: 10 minutes

Serves: 2

Ingredients To Use:

- 1 cup of diced mushroom
- 4 eggs
- Pepper and salt
- ¼ lb of ham
- Buns

Step-by-Step Directions to Cook It:

1. Blend the pecans, flaxseed, and walnut in a blender and set aside
2. Preheat the Hamilton Beach Breakfast Sandwich Maker until the light turns green
3. Open the cover, the top ring, and the cooking plate
4. Sprinkle eggs with pepper and salt, whisk well
5. Put buns on the bottom ring of Hamilton Beach Breakfast Sandwich Maker
6. Top with diced mushrooms, ham
7. Lower the cooking plate and the top ring
8. Put eggs mix the cooking plate, cover with bun
9. Close the cover and cook for 7 minutes
10. Rotate the cooking plate handle clockwise until it stops, serve immediately

Serving suggestion: serve with maple syrup

Preparation and Cooking Tips: dice the mushroom

Nutritional value per serving: Calories: 202kcal, Fat: 4g, Carb: 9g, Proteins: 31g

Almond and Salmon Fillets Sandwich

This is a fantastic recipe with a tempting aroma. It is very easy to make and also less stressful

Preparation time: 5 minutes

 Cooking time: 10 minutes

Serves: 1

Ingredients To Use:

- 1/8 cup of almond meal
- 1 big lemon
- ¼ tsp of ground coriander
- 1 lb of salmon fillet
- ¼ tsp of ground cumin
- Wheat bread slices

Step-by-Step Directions to Cook It:

1. Blend the pecans, flaxseed, and walnut in a blender and set aside
2. Preheat the Hamilton Beach Breakfast Sandwich Maker until the light turns green
3. Open the cover, the top ring, and the cooking plate
4. Put a wheat bread split on the bottom ring of Hamilton Beach Breakfast Sandwich Maker
5. Top with lemon, almond meal
6. Lower the cooking plate and the top ring
7. Put the salmon fillet on the cooking plate, sprinkle cumin and coriander on it, cover with a slice of wheat bread
8. Close the cover and cook for 7 minutes
9. Rotate the cooking plate handle clockwise until it stops, serve immediately

Serving suggestion: serve with cream

Preparation and Cooking Tips: add the salmon skin

Nutritional value per serving: Calories: 223kcal, Fat: 9g, Carb: 10g, Proteins: 25g

Chapter 11: 30-Day Meal Plan

Day 1

Breakfast: Cheese, Egg, and Ham Sandwich

Lunch: South-western Muffin

Dinner: Bacon, cheddar, apple with egg croissant

Day 2

Breakfast: Cheesy egg and sausage bagel

Lunch: Spinach, herb goat cheese with a tomato egg muffin

Dinner: Sausage with pancake

Day 3

Breakfast: Egg, sausage with cheese waffle sandwich

Lunch: English Muffin sandwich

Dinner: Egg benedict sandwich with hollandaise

Day 4

Breakfast: Mozzarella with pesto sun-dried tomato and egg sandwich

Lunch: Grilled cheese sandwich

Dinner: Reuben sandwich

Day 5

Breakfast: Chocolate croissant sandwich

Lunch: Vegetarian panini muffin

Dinner: Stuffed French toast

Day 6

Breakfast: Barbecue brisket burger

Lunch: Barbecue Quesadillas

Dinner: Beer Burger

Day 7

Breakfast: Barbecued Slaw Burger

Lunch: Ground beef burger

Dinner: Beef sandwich

Day 8

Breakfast: Onion marmalade and beef sandwich

Lunch: Bistro beef sandwich

Dinner: Black forest beef sandwich

Day 9

Breakfast: Bleu cheeseburger

Lunch: Brew burger

Dinner: Camel hump sandwich

Day 10

Breakfast: Corned beef sandwich

Lunch: Taco burger

Dinner: Fiesta steak sandwich

Day 11

Breakfast: Asian turkey burger

Lunch: Avocado with chicken sandwich

Dinner: Cajun chicken sandwich

Day 12

Breakfast: Chicken cobb California sandwich

Lunch: Cherry chicken salad sandwich

Dinner: Cordon bleu chicken sandwich

Day 13

Breakfast: Chicken pizza burger

Lunch: Lemony chicken salad sandwich

Dinner: Pita taco chicken pocket

Day 13

Breakfast: Creamy chicken toast burger

Lunch: Dill turkey sandwich

Dinner: Rachel sandwich

Day 14

Breakfast: Reuben Chicken sandwich

Lunch: Jalapeno chicken sandwich

Dinner: Hot brown Kentucky sandwich

Day 15

Breakfast: Alaska salmon salad sandwich

Lunch: Oyster sandwich

Dinner: Boats shrimp sandwich

Day 16

Breakfast: Shrimp hoagie sandwich

Lunch: Shrimp melt sandwich

Dinner: Italian-style shrimp sandwich

Day 17

Breakfast: Crab shell sandwich

Lunch: Tuna Bumsteads burger

Dinner: Tuna cheese spread sandwich

Day 18

Breakfast: Tuna burger

Lunch: Crab melt sandwich

Dinner: Salmon burger

Day 19

Breakfast: Lobster sandwich

Lunch: Acapulco fish burger

Dinner: Egg with parmesan and veggie sandwich

Day 20

Breakfast: Avocado Lettuce Sandwich

Lunch: Chicken Salad Sandwich

Dinner: Club Sandwich

Day 21

Breakfast: Triple-Threat Sandwich

Lunch: Traditional Sandwich

Dinner: Tila sandwich

Day 22

Breakfast: Vegan Philly Sandwich

Lunch: Tomato Sandwich

Dinner: Beet Root Sandwich

Day 23

Breakfast: Vegan Sloppy Joes

Lunch: Cookie Nuttela Snack

Dinner: Cinnamon sandwich

Day 24

Breakfast: Butter almond muffin

Lunch: Fig Flavored Croissant

Dinner: Peanut Veggie Sandwich

Day 25

Breakfast: Butter almond muffin

Lunch: Coconut Peach Sandwich

Dinner: Cinnamon sandwich

Day 26

Breakfast: Butter almond muffin

Lunch: Western omelet classic

Dinner: Green Sandwich

Day 27

Breakfast: Butter almond muffin

Lunch: Blueberry Croissants

Dinner: Hamilton Chive Sandwich

Day 28

Breakfast: BLT Sandwich

Lunch: Creamy Waffles

Dinner: Slaw Muffins

Day 29

Breakfast: Reuben Vegan Sandwich

Lunch: Ham and Omelet Sandwich

Dinner: Marshmellow Toast

Day 30

Breakfast: Hamilton Cheese Sandwich

Lunch: Cheese Bagel and Buttered Egg

Dinner: Steak Stuffed Pancake Sandwich

Conclusion

Successful Family picnics, social gatherings, friendly hangouts, and light lunch packs are just a Hamilton Beach Breakfast Sandwich Maker away. The appliance is simply a must-have for everyone. And this cookbook is the right choice for remarkable meals with the Hamilton Beach Breakfast Sandwich Maker

Good Luck!

CPSIA information can be obtained
at www.ICGtesting.com
Printed in the USA
LVHW062236051121
702531LV00004B/403